W9-BMD-259

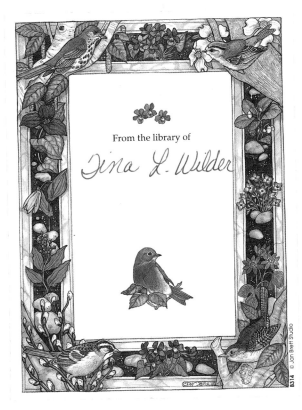

From the library of

Tina L. Wilder

THE
NEEDLEWORK
GARDEN

THE NEEDLEWORK GARDEN

Inspiring Designs for Creative Embroidery

JANE ILES

Chronicle Books · San Francisco

To My Parents

Art Director Cherriwyn Magill
Photographs by Julie Fisher
Styling by Jackie Boase
Illustrations by Sally Holmes
Charts by John Hutchinson

Printed and bound in Italy
by New Interlitho, Spa

Library of Congress Cataloging in Publication Data
Iles, Jane.
The needlework garden / by Jane Iles.
p.   cm.
Includes index.
ISBN 0-87701-633-X
1. Needlework—Patterns.   2. Decoration and ornament—Plant forms.
3. Flowers in art.   4. Gardens in art.   I. Title.
TT753.I43   1989
746.44—dc19   88-38327
CIP

10 9 8 7 6 5 4 3 2 1

Chronicle Books
275 Fifth Street
San Francisco, California
94103

contents

i n t r o d u c t i o n

*e*mbroidery, which is the embellishment by stitchery of fabric with additional pattern, colour and texture, has been practised all over the world for many centuries. Evidence of historical decorative needlework can still be seen today in the many and varied artifacts preserved since ancient Egyptian times.

Practised by both rich and poor people, it has been used throughout history to create beautiful items which may be functional as well as ornamental. Today it is enjoying a great revival in popularity and can be seen in a huge variety of forms.

Similarly, the craft of gardening has developed throughout the world for thousands of years. Indeed, it is thought that the inventors of gardening were the people of the New Stone Age, not less than 7,000 years ago. They worked with simple tools such as digging sticks, grew plants in orderly straight lines, dug irrigation channels and erected protective fences, all of which are evidence of planning and careful design, rather than random cultivation.

Flower gardens were not of great importance in earliest times, since the emphasis was laid upon the production of food crops and medicinal plants. However, there is evidence of lilies being grown for their beautiful flowers, and soon an interest developed in the arrangement of various plants for their different visual effects.

The main function of the garden today, whether in a rural or urban setting, is to give pleasure and to provide a place for relaxation. However, it must not be forgotten that to many people a garden is still the important provider of food crops.

To bring the two crafts of embroidery and gardening together in this book has been both stimulating and enjoyable. The gardens have provided inspiration for the designs and the embroidery is the means of expressing them.

You will find a great variety of ideas. Some are quick and easy to reproduce, while others require more time, skill and patience. All will enhance the home and give pleasure to both the maker and the observer, and it is hoped that they will stimulate readers to develop and express their own thoughts and ideas on this intriguing subject.

Jane Lees.

cottage gardens

*Nostalgic thoughts of cottage gardens filled with
old-fashioned plants have provided the ideas for
these delightful mirror and picture frames.*

a popular image of a cottage garden may be the abundance of brilliant colours, sweet scents, rambling plants and regimented rows of vegetables, all enclosed within sturdy walls or thicket-like hedges. Indeed, this is an idyllic view which many readers would love to possess, and one into which they would like to be able to step at will.

Healthy young plants growing side by side with ancient neighbours all provide vibrant colours at some time during the year. Lupins, hollyhocks, briar roses, poppies, daisies, dahlias all spring to mind. The cottage garden is perhaps the most inspiring of all gardens for the needleworker.

One of the most charming aspects of the cottage garden is a sense of organized chaos, with huge clumps of plants all jostling for space in a relatively small area. In the past, time was short for the majority of cottage gardeners. Years ago, the owner snatched short breaks to tend the garden between spells at work nearby. Today the garden may only be tended at weekends, with the owner either commuting great distances to work daily or living and working somewhere else during the week. So the plants have always had to look after themselves to a certain extent. They needed to be strong and sturdy in order to flourish and grow successfully.

Today, it is encouraging to see that many of the plants that our great-grandparents may have known are being cultivated once more by plant breeders, making these beautiful species available to us all again.

h o l l y h o c k   b a t h   l i n e n

One of the most striking plants associated with cottage gardens is the hollyhock. It has been grown for centuries, changing little over the years and giving tall displays of beautiful flowers, which range from bright crimson to muted creams and white.

The border design which has been used to decorate this hand towel and washcloth has been inspired by the hollyhock, showing the softly changing colours of bud to flower and the lush foliage and strong stems. The bumble bees have been added as they would surely be present in any cottage garden where these beautiful flowers might be seen.

materials

1 cream hand towel, approximately
  56cm (22in) wide
1 30cm (12in) square washcloth
20cm (8in) piece of cream cotton
  polyester fabric, 90cm (36in) wide
20cm (8in) piece of white cotton
  polyester fabric, 90cm (36in) wide
Pale green sewing thread
Cream sewing thread
1 skein each Anchor stranded

embroidery thread:
Spray 1: 6, 328, 337, 778, 264, 266
Spray 2: 103, 893, 895, 968, 260, 262
Spray 3: 25, 48, 76, 892, 213, 216
Centre flowers 305
Bumble bees 306, 393, 905
Tracing paper
15cm (6in) wooden embroidery hoop
Green, pink, brown crayons

to work the embroidered border and corner motif

1. Either trace the border design three times, joining the design in a long strip, or make three photocopies of it and join the pieces together. Trim to the width of your towel plus 2cm ($\frac{3}{4}$in) turning allowance. Trace the corner design on a small piece of tracing paper.

2. Press the cream and white fabrics to remove any creases.

Attach the design pattern strip to a clean, flat surface with tape. Similarly anchor the cream fabric centrally over one end of it and then slip the corner design under the other end of the

REMEMBER TO ALLOW FABRIC BETWEEN TWO DESIGNS

fabric. Accurately trace the design straight on the fabric using the coloured crayons (remember to keep the points well-sharpened). Do not trace the yellow centres or the dotted guide lines on the fabric (see left).

3. Place the white backing fabric under the cream fabric, and use Diagonal Basting Stitches to hold the two layers together (see Special Techniques, page 134).

Place the fabrics in the embroidery hoop, pulling the layers gently around the hoop to achieve a taut working area.

4. Use three strands of embroidery thread at all times unless otherwise directed.

If you look at the border design, you will see that it is made up of two long hollyhock sprays which gently twist around each other. However, you have three sets of coloured threads with which to work the design. This will create a more interesting effect as the repeat pattern becomes less obvious than if you use only two sets of colours.

5. Working with one set of colours,

With care you can work the border and corner designs together on the one piece of fabric, and with the use of the different sets of coloured threads, the repeat pattern becomes more interesting.

Use this simplified hollyhock spray for the corner motif of the washcloth.

GUIDE LINE FOR MACHINED BORDER

15

GUIDE LINE FOR MACHINED BORDER

Above, two gently twisting hollyhock sprays have been arranged to form a continuous pattern. The half stems on each side of the centre spray join to become the second spray when the design is repeated and joined together.

Right, each open flower has a circlet of closely spaced Buttonhole Stitches surrounding the star-like centre which is worked in radiating Straight Stitch.

Opposite, different embroidery stitches are used to emphasize the various parts of the design.

begin with the flowers. The small buds are all worked in Satin Stitch in the two palest shades of each set. Then work circlets of closely spaced Buttonhole Stitch around the open flowers, gradually changing from the paler shades to the two stronger shades, leaving the centres of each flower unworked. Fill each flower centre with Yellow 305, working small Straight Stitches to give a star-like centre (see right).

The leaves are worked in Encroaching Straight Stitches, working from the jagged edges in towards the centre, filling the leaf shapes completely. Then the stem is worked in lines of Back Stitch which are placed close together side by side to give a solid, thick line.

6. Embroider the bumble bees, starting with the wings. Use only two strands of Light Brown 393 to work tiny Back Stitches along the edges of

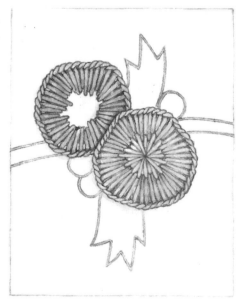

the wings and the fine veins. Then using three strands, work the Dark Brown 905 antennae, legs and bands around the body in tiny Straight Stitches. Finally, work bands of Gold

REPEAT

306 across the body between the dark brown bands.

7. Reposition the embroidery hoop as necessary. Using the other two sets of colours and repeating the three sets as necessary, repeat the process of using the palest colours for the upper parts of the sprays, and the brighter colours for the lower, mature parts.

8. Work the small corner motif in a similar way, selecting one of the three sets of colours to use.

9. Remove the fabric from the embroidery hoop and press on the wrong side to remove any creases. Carefully remove all basting threads.

10. Follow the dotted guide lines to cut out the paper pattern for the corner motif and place it over the embroidered version. Lightly draw around the pattern outline using the green crayon. Similarly cut out and use the long design strip to mark the straight edges of the border.

If your sewing machine makes embroidery stitches, choose a suitable one and stitch with pale green sewing thread along the crayoned guide lines of the border strip and the corner motif. (If your machine does not do machine embroidery, you can work a simple closed Zigzag Stitch along the lines). With sharp-pointed scissors, trim away the surplus fabric around the corner motif and along the edges of the border. Cut across the short ends of the border to fit the towel, allowing a 1cm (⅜in) turning at each end.

Pin and baste the border strip across one end of the towel and the motif on one corner of the face cloth. Then work an open zigzag machine stitch along the edges of the embroidered fabric.

Slip Stitch the ends of the border strip to the sides of the towel using cream sewing thread.

The thickness of embroidery thread is reduced to two strands when working the delicate wings of the bumble bees.

cottage garden mirror frame

The soft, smoky colours of old-fashioned cottage garden flowers have inspired this pretty mirror frame. The flowers and leaves are all made of felt shapes edged in Buttonhole Stitch, and the variations of the different colours have been created by using slightly different shades of wool yarn.

The mirror frame could easily be adapted to use with a favourite picture or photograph simply by replacing the mirror with a piece of cardboard and the subject of your choice.

materials

18cm (7¼in) diameter circular mirror
25cm (10in) square of pale green felt
Small amounts of sage green felt, pale blue felt, pale mauve felt, flesh pink felt
25 × 50cm (10 × 20in) piece of heavyweight interfacing
25cm (10in) square of suitable printed cotton fabric

Paterna Persian yarn: 1 skein Loden Green 692; small amounts of Peacock Green 687; Shamrock 622; Olive Green 653; Plum 322, 324; Fuchsia 350; Ginger 883, 885; Salmon 846; Wood Rose 924; Glacier 564
Flesh pink and pale green sewing thread
Clear glue suitable for fabric and glass
Small curtain ring

to make the cottage garden frame

1. Place the circular mirror over one half of the heavyweight interfacing and draw around it. Then place the mirror over the other half and draw around it once more. Add 0.6cm (¼in) all around to each circle. Cut out each piece on the outer line to give the basis of your fabric frame.

2. Place the floral fabric right side downwards on a clean flat surface. Place one of the interfacing circles over the fabric and pin the two layers

Previous page, bumble bees hover around hollyhock flowers in this finely embroidered design, to make a very special set of bath linen.

together. Trim the floral fabric, leaving a 1cm (⅜in) turning allowance. With sewing thread, baste the turning to the wrong side of the circle of interfacing without stitching through to the right side of the floral fabric.

3. Draw a smaller circle 1.2cm (½in) inside the edge of the second interfacing frame circle. Cut away the centre circle, leaving the narrow frame intact.

4. Place this frame on top of the pale green felt square and pin the two layers together carefully without distorting the quite flimsy circular shape. Trim away the excess felt, leaving a 1cm (⅜in) allowance around the frame. Baste this narrow turning to the back of the frame without stitching through to the right side of the felt. Trim turned edge if necessary. Then carefully cut away the centre of the green felt, again leaving 1cm (⅜in) turning. Baste this inner turning to the wrong

side of the frame. There is no need to snip the turning in towards the interfacing shape because the felt will stretch if gently eased out to fit.

5. Using the pale pink sewing thread with your sewing machine set to a wide Satin Stitch (closed Zigzag Stitch), work an even line of stitching around the edge of the back of the frame (the floral fabric circle), approximately 0.6cm (¼in) away from the edge. Similarly work a line of Satin Stitch around the centre of the narrow front frame (the green felt circle).

6. Using the leaf and flower shapes as a guide, cut out nine small single leaves and five leaf clusters from the sage green felt; four pale green leaf clusters; four large and four small mauve flower shapes; three large and three small blue flower shapes and two large and two small pink flower shapes. (When cutting out the small

Subtle changes in the shade of yarn soften the colour of the felt flowers when Buttonhole Stitch is worked around their edges.

Trace-off patterns for the leaves and flowers.

Work the Chain Stitch line so that it appears to twist around the machined Satin Stitching.

flowers, some can have four petals and some have five petals.)

7. Use a single strand of Persian yarn at all times.

Use the Peacock Green 687 and Shamrock 622 to work small, evenly spaced Buttonhole Stitch around the pale green leaf clusters. When you have worked around all the leaves on a cluster, gather the centre slightly by working Running Stitches around the centre and pulling the thread gently before fastening the thread securely.

Work the sage green leaf clusters in the same way using Loden Green 692 and Olive Green 653 yarn. Then work the tiny single leaves in Loden Green 692.

Work the same evenly spaced Buttonhole Stitch around the flower shapes, gathering the centres more tightly so that they appear fuller than the leaves. Use Plum 322 and 324 for the mauve flower pieces; Salmon 846 and Wood Rose 924 for the flesh pink flower pieces; and finally Glacier 564 and Plum 324 for the blue flower pieces. (Use the stronger colours for the larger flower pieces.)

8. Pin each small flower piece on top of a larger flower piece of the same

coloured felt and place them on top of a leaf cluster. Then arrange the leaves and flowers along a 20cm (8in) section of the narrow, green felt front frame.

You can arrange the flowers as seen in the illustration or in your own way. When you are satisfied with the arrangement, invisibly and securely hand sew them in position using pale green sewing thread. Then using Fuchsia 350, Ginger 883 and 885, work a French Knot of each colour in the centre of all the flowers.

9. Using Loden Green 692, work a line of small neat Chain Stitches around the remaining part of the frame, gently curving it around the line of machine stitching, stopping and starting it at the line of machine stitching so that it looks as if it goes behind the Satin Stitching (see below). Then arrange the small single leaves evenly along the curving Chain Stitch and carefully sew them in place using matching yarn. Using Fuchsia 350, Ginger 883 and 885 again, work a French Knot of each colour at the

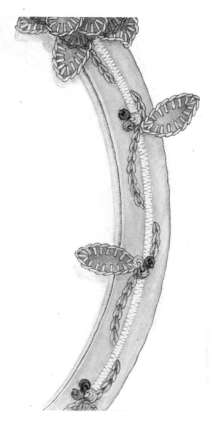

The frame can be used to hold a picture instead of a mirror.

base of each tiny leaf.

10. Place the back and front frame pieces together and pin to hold. Stitch the curtain ring centrally near the top of the back of the frame.

11. With a double pale green sewing thread, Slip Stitch the two edges of the frame pieces together. You can work around half of the frame before inserting the mirror in position. Complete the stitching to hold the mirror in place.

With a little clear adhesive, very carefully glue the frame rim to the mirror neatly to complete the project.

If you have a mirror of a different shape or size that you would like to use, you can easily make your own frame simply by using the mirror as a template and enlarging the pattern shape by at least 0.6cm ($\frac{1}{4}$in) all around. (If the mirror is thick, allow extra around the shape.) Then use this pattern to estimate how much fabric you will need.

If you wish to make a picture frame instead of a mirror frame, choose a photograph or picture to mount within the frame and follow the same guidelines.

the
formal
garden

*Strong shapes and colours emphasize two different
aspects of the formal garden, the detail of the tub
and the pattern of the knot garden.*

g eometric patterns of immaculate lawns, paths and ornamental flower-beds make up the formal garden, which was so popular in the sixteenth and seventeenth centuries in Europe. Labour was plentiful and grand ideas and dreams became reality in many magnificent gardens, for example Versailles. We can still see many of these gardens, which are now open to the public.

On a more modest scale, the modern landscape architect has created areas in the urban environment where concrete and pavements are interspersed with formal beds of flowers and shrubs.

k n o t   g a r d e n   c u s h i o n

The knot garden, which is a rare but beautiful sight today, is the theme for this colourful canvaswork cushion, which has a variety of textured backgrounds and, applied on top of these, small felt flowers and leaves. The design is a naive interpretation, although the strong geometric pattern is typical of such a garden.

Knot gardens were particularly popular in England in the sixteenth and seventeenth centuries, when domestic gardens were planned and laid out in geometric patterns. Beds of sweet-smelling flowers were enclosed by neat, low hedges of thyme, lavender and other small, shrubby herbs. Narrow paths formed the entwining patterns around these beds, which were seen at their best when looked down on from the windows of the owner's home.

m a t e r i a l s

45cm (18in) square of single thread canvas – 6 threads per cm (14 threads per in)

Paterna Persian yarns: 3 skeins Shamrock 624; 4 skeins Spring Green 635; 5 skeins each Peacock Green 685 and 687; 3 skeins Cream 261; 3 skeins Pale Flesh 493; 1 skein each Flesh Pink 490; Cranberry 945; Ice Blue 555, 553

36cm (14in) square of small printed cotton fabric to complement (for back of cushion).

White sewing thread

15cm (6in) square of felt in each of the following colours: pale pink, pale blue, pale green and peacock green

33cm (13in) square cushion pad

Waterproof or indelible marking pen

Wooden embroidery frame to stretch canvas on

t o   m a k e   t h e   k n o t   g a r d e n   c u s h i o n

1. Draw the complete garden design on a sheet of tracing paper using the trace-off pattern which gives a quarter section of it. Place it on a flat surface and align the piece of canvas over it, matching the straight lines of the

Different stitches are used to create a variety of background textures. Simple appliquéd flowers and leaves complete the design.

design with the threads of the canvas. With masking tape, temporarily hold the paper and canvas together on the flat surface. Then carefully draw the design on the canvas using the waterproof marking pen. Leave the canvas for an hour to make sure the ink is thoroughly dry. Mount the canvas on the embroidery frame.

2. You are now ready to begin stitching.

Work with two strands of yarn throughout. It does not really matter which area you work first, but leave the hedges of French Knots until last. The centre circle and outer curved borders are worked in Dutch Cross Stitch, which is a simple combination of an oblong Cross Stitch and a vertical Straight Stitch. The five areas are covered with this stitch in Cream and Pale Flesh yarn (see right). Have two needles threaded with the two yarns so that you can work the colours simultaneously to create a random pattern.

To make the stitch, work the oblong Cross Stitches first, working over four vertical and two horizontal threads. Fit the second row into the first and then the third row will fit below the second so that the oblong Cross Stitches of the third row are in line with those of the first row (see right).

Do not work the vertical Straight Stitches until the Cross Stitches have all been made. Then, bring the needle out one horizontal thread above the centre of each cross. The yarn is then

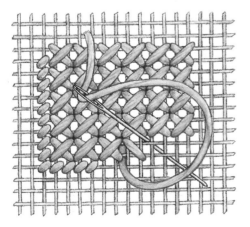

taken down over four horizontal threads. If you find the stitches are too large to fit the shape of the design neatly, fill in the gaps with small Tent Stitches (half Cross Stitches).

The four corner areas, which are squares with an arched hedge through them, are simply worked in Shamrock Green Cross Stitch, working each stitch over two intersections of canvas. Remember that the upper stitch of each cross must always be made in the same direction (see below left). Again, if you find the size of the cross is not quite right for the shape of the area being filled, fill the gap with small Tent Stitches (see below left).

Dutch Cross Stitch: once you have worked the first row of oblong cross stitches, you will find the next line falls into place quite easily. Two colours of yarn are used simultaneously to produce a random effect.

The four areas surrounding the centre circle are all worked so that they look like grass. Each section is worked with the long straight stitches pointing towards the centre. The stitch used is called Encroaching Straight Stitch. It is worked freely in lines of stitches of varying length, with each line fitting into the previous one. Remember not to make each stitch more than 1.5cm ($\frac{5}{8}$in); as long stitches could be snagged, they are impractical for this cushion design (see overleaf). Use the Spring Green yarn to work these areas.

To complete these grassy patches of the garden, scatter French Knots over them using a single strand of Cranberry.

To complete the background, fill in the hedge pattern, working in a com-

Cross Stitch: work all the Cross Stitches in the same direction and if you find that they do not fill the areas exactly, then fill any gaps with small Tent Stitches.

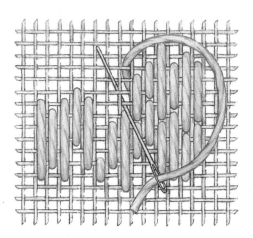

Encroaching Straight Stitch: this gives a random effect ideal for the grassy areas of the design. (It is also very useful where subtle shading is required such as on petals or leaves.)

bination of the two Peacock Green yarns, using a single strand of each shade in the needle at the same time to give a speckled effect.

Work massed areas of French Knots to create a very rich and raised effect. You will find it easier and much more effective to work a row of French Knots on each side of the shapes to be filled and then work extra knots in between to cover the canvas. They do not have to form a neat pattern as long as they make a rich and solid hedge.

3. Now the background of your Knot Garden is complete.

Cut out twenty-four leaves from both shades of green felt, then cut out twenty-four pink and blue flowers (see trace-off opposite).

Use a single strand of yarn for all the following embroidery.

Work small neat Blanket Stitch around each of the circles. Work sixteen Cranberry Pink flowers, four Pale Flesh and four Flesh Pink flowers. Similarly work around the blue felt circles; make twelve each using the two shades of Ice Blue yarn.

Arrange the flowers and leaves on the canvas using the green yarns as indicated (see opposite). Work the stems of the flowers in neat Chain Stitches in the same colour that is used to attach the leaves to the background in Back Stitch.

To attach all the flowers, work three French Knots in the centre of each felt circle using the two Peacock shades and the Spring Green. These create a bright, eye-catching centre in each flower.

Remove the canvas from the frame. Trim the canvas, leaving a 1.5cm ($\frac{5}{8}$in) seam allowance around the stitchery.

4. With right sides together, pin, baste and machine stitch the cushion face and back together. Leave a gap along one side of approximately 20cm (8in). Trim the excess fabric at the corners before turning to the right side. Fill with the cushion pad. Neatly turn in the edges of the opening and close with tiny Slip Stitches.

keepsake cards

Everyone appreciates a handmade greetings card. It means so much more than an ordinary card, as it has been made with loving care.

These cards can be made with only a small amount of material and a little time and patience. But they will give the receiver great pleasure, and they will ensure that your message is successfully given, whether it is 'Happy Birthday', 'Get Well', or 'Best Wishes'.

Once given, they can be framed to make an everlasting keepsake.

The empty cards can be purchased in packs from good craft shops and are

available in a variety of sizes and colours. They also have different shaped cut-outs such as circles, hearts, squares and ovals. If you have difficulty in obtaining these readymade cards, you can make your own quite easily (see Special Techniques, page 136).

materials for each card

1 card 15.75 × 11cm (6¼ × 4¼in) with rectangular cut-out
Small amounts of DMC Coton Perlé thread No. 5:

To draw the complete design, you need not trace all the details, but only the green parallel lines of the hedge pattern. Then use the pink dotted lines to help you match up each quarter accurately.

Made with only a little time and effort, a hand-worked card will always mean more than a mass-produced one.

Card with brick wall: Green 906, 954; Yellow 743; Orange 741; Pink 894; Ecru; Brown 407, 433

Card with paving stones: Green 472, 993; Mauve 209; Pink 605, 718; Ecru; Brown 407, 433

Card with trellis: Green 469, 907; Red 606; Blue 799; Mauve 554; Ecru; Brown 407, 433

15cm (6in) square white (synthetic or mixture) linen-type fabric

15cm (6in) square white backing fabric

1 packet fabric transfer crayons (Crayola)

12.5cm (5in) embroidery hoop

Clear adhesive glue suitable for fabric and card

Small piece of tracing paper

to make the keepsake cards

The three cards are all based on one design of a Versailles tub with a small tree which could be a bay tree or a small standard fuchsia or rose.

Masses of trailing foliage and small flowering plants are at the foot of the tree spilling over onto the ground.

Each card is worked in the same way, but relies on a different combination of colours to make it look a little different from the others.

The use of fabric transfer crayons is put to advantage in this project, as it gives an instant design on the fabric upon which to stitch. Areas of the design have been left unstitched to show the crayoning on the fabric.

1. Place a small piece of tracing paper over the trace-off pattern and transfer

The form of the Versailles tub is shown by working areas of Satin Stitch in different directions. The sheen of the thread also helps.

the design lines onto it. Then turn it over so that you can crayon in the underside of it using the transfer crayons and looking at the coloured drawing to guide you. Test the strength of the crayons if you have not used them before, as sometimes they can produce very strong colours if used heavily.

The main differences are the colours of the flowers and whether you want a trellis, brick wall or paving stones around your Versailles tub. (You can mix different components of the design rather than reproduce one exactly the same as those shown here.)

2. Press the white linen-type fabric to remove any creases. Allow it to cool completely before placing the crayonned design face downwards onto the fabric. (If you place the paper on the warm fabric, the warmth of the fabric will cause the crayon marks to smudge.) Transfer the design onto the fabric using the hot iron (follow the manufacturer's instructions).

Make sure the tracing paper does not move on the fabric while you transfer the design, as this will cause blurring and a smudged effect.

Your coloured design is now on the fabric. Decide whether you want very strong colours or much softer, paler ones. If your design is very bright on the fabric you may want a different

selection of coloured threads. This project is ideal to try using dye crayons, because if you do not like the results you can easily try again as only a small piece of fabric is used.

Remember to brush or blow off any excess specks of crayon on your paper, before transferring the design to the fabric, as they will also be transferred and spoil your design.

3. Place the design and the backing fabric together in the hoop, pulling the layers gently to achieve a taut working area within the hoop.

4. Work the main stem or trunk of the tree in Dark Brown 433 Satin Stitches to achieve a thick and solid effect.

Work the Versailles tub in Ecru Satin Stitches, making the sides and corner pieces stand out from one another by positioning the stitches in different directions (see below left).

Work the trellis, brick wall or paving stones in Chocolate Brown 407 Back Stitch along the design lines to give a suggestion of what surrounds the tub.

Work the foliage of the tree in a combination of the two shades of green, working clumps of Single Chain Stitches so that they look like lots of leaves. Then add small Dark Brown 433 Straight Stitches to represent the twigs and branches that are just visible between the leaves. Then work lots of French Knots tightly clustered together over the righthand side of the tub where there are lots of small plants growing. Use a mixture of the three flower colours, unless you are working the design with the red flowers; work Red 606 French Knots in definite clumps like geranium flowers and also a few Red 606 Knots at the base of the tub. Then scatter the Blue 799 and Mauve 554 Knots over the trailing plants.

Work the foliage in Single Chain Stitches, choosing one shade of green for the trailing plants and one for the flowering plants. (You can mix them if you wish.)

Add a few French Knots to the tree

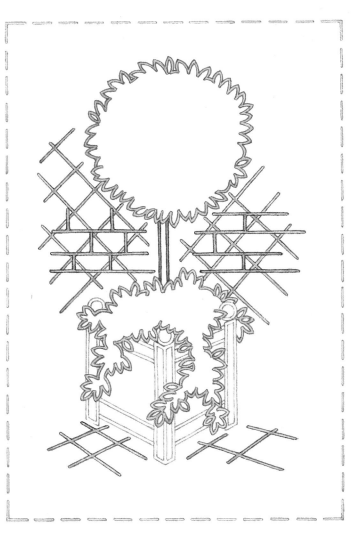

to represent flowers or berries to make it look more colourful.

5. When you have completed the stitchery, remove the fabric from the hoop and press it on the wrong side to remove any creases and to encourage the stitchery to have an embossed effect.

6. Open the card out flat and place the cut-out section of it over the embroidered design. Estimate how much fabric has to be cut away, and trim the surplus so that the design fits within the frame but allows a border to overlap and be glued to the card.

Use the clear glue to hold the design centrally within the cut-out frame and then fold the backing section over the wrong side of the design and glue them together to complete the keepsake card.

Choose which background detail you want before drawing the design onto tracing paper, then lightly use the fabric transfer crayons.

t h e   h e r b
g a r d e n

The pretty gillyflowers have transformed the plain bed linen, while above hangs a delightful window garden picture which is worked in a variety of techniques.

*t*he herb garden is enjoying a great revival in interest, and there are many fine examples to be seen today, particularly in the British Isles. They have a long and varied history dating back to medieval times, when herbs were formally divided into two growing areas by the monks: one for culinary and the other for medicinal purposes.

Herbs were grown first in simple beds or strips for the convenience of the gatherer, not for the pleasure of a spectator, but the Elizabethan gardener was interested in using his plants decoratively as well, and the simple monastic strips gave way to attractive patterns and designs. Depending upon the creativity of the gardener, the herb garden became a delightful geometric arrangement of intricately interwoven paths and beds.

The popularity of the herb garden waned during the period of the landscape garden, until early in this century when there was a revival in the use of culinary herbs, which in turn led to a revival and rediscovery of herbal cultivation.

Today, it is possible to grow a wide range of herbs. Seed merchants offer more and more varieties to the customer, who has many different options for growing a choice of herbs – pots of chives and parsley on a high-rise balcony can provide as much enjoyment as the corner in a large country garden laid out in an interesting pattern.

h e r b   g a r d e n   c u s h i o n

To complete the cushion, a piped velvet edging is added and purple and pink corner tassels echo the colours of the herbs.

This beautiful cushion with its subtle combination of colours has been inspired by a typical pattern that could have been used in an Elizabethan herb garden.

Criss-crossing footpaths separating areas of soil create tiny flowerbeds, and carefully planned rows of plants such as lavender, chives or pinks provide the framework of the design.

It has been worked entirely in Straight Stitch and French Knots, relying on colour, size and direction of stitching to create the desired effect.

The design has been made into a cushion which has been enhanced by a green velvet edging with tiny tassels at each corner. It would be equally effective to make the design into a framed wall picture. To make a scented herb pillow to go with this cushion, work just the centre star pattern and fill the pillow with herbs to give it a delicate fragrance.

m a t e r i a l s

2 50cm (20in) squares of beige cotton fabric
1 50 cm (20in) square of white cotton backing fabric
DMC Coton Perlé thread No. 5: 2 skeins each Beige 738, 543; 1 skein each Green 369, 954, 912, 3348, 907; Mauve 210, 208; Pink 605, 718, 818

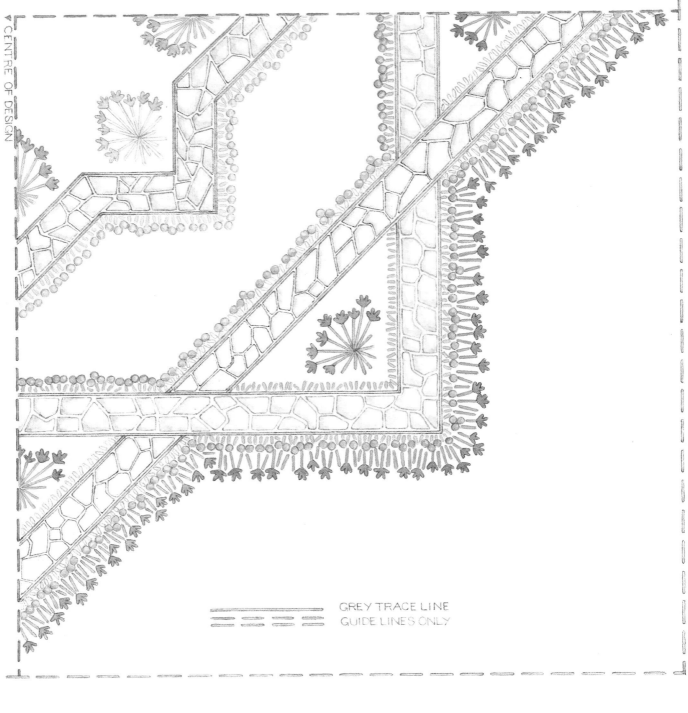

CENTRE OF DESIGN

GREY TRACE LINE
GUIDE LINES ONLY

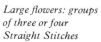 *Paths: groups of Satin Stitches*

 Large flowers: groups of three or four Straight Stitches

Small flowers: French Knots

Grass: uneven Straight Stitches

Plants: long Straight Stitches meeting in a centre point

543	3348
738	208
912	210
954	718
369	605
907	818

Draw only the grey trace lines onto your paper pattern and fabric.

The very simple interpretation of the herbs into stitchery and the finely detailed crazy paving footpaths effectively complement each other, and are emphasized by the surrounding areas of plain fabric.

1.5m (60in) green velvet ribbon, 1.5cm (⅝in) wide
3m (3¼yd) double knitting wool (knitting worsted yarn)
Green sewing thread
34cm (13½in) square cushion pad
34cm (13½in) tracing paper
Fabric transfer pencil or dressmakers' carbon paper
40cm (16in) square wooden frame (approximate size)

to make the herb garden cushion

1. Fold the tracing paper in half and half again into quarter sections. Open it out and mark the centre and along the fold lines. Then, using these as guidelines, place the paper over the trace-off pattern, matching them up with the dotted guidelines of the pattern. Accurately draw the footpaths a quarter at a time until you have a complete design that joins up.

If your beige fabric is thin enough to see through, trace the design directly on one of the squares of fabric. If, however, it is not transparent enough, use either a fabric transfer pencil or dressmakers' carbon paper (follow the manufacturer's instructions) to transfer the design. Remember to place it centrally on the beige fabric and align one set of parallel lines with the straight grain of the fabric.

2. Stretch the backing fabric and then the beige fabric on the wooden frame, making sure the design lines are straight.

3. Use the trace-off pattern as a guide to work the embroidery.

Begin by building up the geometric pattern of the paths. These are worked in groups of Straight Stitches (Satin Stitches) which are evenly and quite closely spaced, so that they appear as individual paving stones. There is no definitive way to work the paths, but it is more effective if you vary both the direction of stitching and the shape of each paving stone. The lustre of the Coton Perlé thread gives a rich effect in the light when worked in different directions.

The outer paths are each worked entirely in one shade of Beige 738 or 543, but mix the two shades together when working the middle path.

4. Work tiny rows of Straight Stitches in the appropriate shade of Green around the footpaths, varying the size and angle of each stitch so that they look like grassy foliage.

5. Then, using the appropriate shade of Pink and Mauve, work groups of tiny French Knots along the grassy lines, again varying their positions and spacing. Remember there is no line of grass and flowers along the longer side of the small triangles that are formed by the pattern of the paths, nor along the inner edge of the middle path.

6. Work a second row of Straight Stitches around the outside edge of the footpath pattern using the two deeper shades of Green. These stitches can be longer and spaced further apart.

7. At the ends of these longer Straight Stitches, work three or four tiny Straight Stitches, using the deeper Pink and Mauve to form the flowers. You do not have to work a flower at the end of each green stitch, but try to group them and space them to form a pleasing effect.

8. Work the larger plants in the triangular spaces and also in the corners of the middle footpath using the appropriate shade of Green thread. These are made by working several long Straight Stitches that all converge in a centre point. They should be of differing lengths and the ones on the lower half of the plant should be shorter than those on the upper half.

9. On the ends of the upper 'stems' of these plants, work tiny Straight Stitch flowers, using the appropriate colour of thread in the same way as you worked them around the outer footpaths to complete the design.

10. Remove the embroidered fabric from the frame. Using your tracing of the design, lightly mark the seam line

Opposite, do not draw the dotted lines onto the fabric. They are to help you keep the repeat pattern straight while preparing it.

with tailor's chalk and trim away the excess fabric, leaving a 1.5cm ($\frac{5}{8}$in) seam allowance on each side.

11. Make the velvet edging. Fold the ribbon in half and machine stitch along the entire length of it, keeping the line of stitching approximately 3mm ($\frac{1}{8}$in) away from the edge to form a narrow channel. Pass a double length of knitting yarn through the channel to pad the ribbon out slightly. Pin, baste and machine stitch this around the cushion front, matching the line of stitching on the ribbon with the marked seam line. Join and finish the ends of the ribbon as neatly as possible to prevent them from fraying

and to make the edging appear continuous. Then pin and baste the cushion pieces together and accurately machine stitch them together along the line of stitching which holds the velvet edging in position. Extra care must be taken at the corners.

Leave an opening along one side.

12. Make four tassels using the Deep Pink 718 thread and four of the Deep Mauve 208 (see Special Techniques, page 135), and sew one of each colour to each corner of the cushion.

13. Insert the pad into the cushion cover, and with small neat Slip Stitches, close the opening to complete your herb garden cushion.

g i l l y f l o w e r   b e d   l i n e n

The position of each stitch is important as it not only shows the colour, but also the shape and form of the plant.

Gillyflowers are more widely known as dianthus, but are also called pinks or border carnations.

The sweet, heavy scent that they produce in the summer months even inspired the name of 'Clove July' flowers, which was recorded by William Lawson in 1617 in his book *The Countrie Housewifes Garden*.

There have been references to this pretty flower and its uses as a herb since the fourth century BC, when it is believed to have been given its Greek name, dianthus, which literally means 'flower of the gods'.

From its origins in southern Europe, it was taken to Great Britain by the Normans and one of its popular uses in Tudor times was to give a spicy flavour to wine.

Today, it is a popular perennial available in many shades of pink, and is seen providing bright splashes of colour in flowerbeds rather than in the herb garden. The flowers can be used in salads, preserves and of course in pot pourri.

In this project, you can see how a few sprigs of the gillyflower have been used to build up a pretty repeat pattern which decorates a pillowcase and single bed sheet. If you wish, you could work the same design across a bedcover or double bedsheet or along the hemmed edge of bedroom curtains and bath linen instead.

materials

Pale pink cotton polyester single bed (flat) sheet and matching pillowcase
Anchor stranded embroidery thread:
1 skein each Yellow 301; Pink 63; Green 259; 2 skeins each Green 216, 214, 266; Pink 50, 60, 75, 893
25cm (10in) diameter wooden embroidery hoop
Pink and green crayons

to make gillyflower bed linen

NB: If you intend to decorate more than the single sheet and one pillowcase, remember that you may need extra embroidery thread.

1. Make a tracing of the gillyflower sprigs; from this make a reverse tracing. Make two photocopies of the original tracing and one of the reverse tracing.

Trim away the surplus paper on both sides of the dotted lines on the pattern and carefully join the strips together, alternating the original and reverse patterns so that they join and overlap in a pleasing way to make the repeat pattern.

(You only need to prepare a strip of three repeats for the pillowcase and single sheet, but you will need more for a double sheet.)

2. Press the pillowcase and sheet to remove any creases.

Place the pillowcase on a clean flat surface. Fold the repeat pattern so that only two complete repeats are seen, then carefully place the strip inside the pillowcase until it is only 5cm (2in) away from the closed end. Pin it in position. Then with sharp-pointed pink and green crayons, trace the sprigs of gillyflowers straight onto the fabric.

Remember to keep the points of the crayons sharpened as you work because thick ugly lines would spoil the delicate design.

GUIDE LINES TO ENSURE PATTERN IS STRAIGHT

POSITION OF REPEAT REVERSED

3. When you have completed the tracing, remove the paper strip from inside the pillowcase. Unfold the strip so that the three repeats are seen. Then find the centre of the 'fold over' edge of the sheet (the edge with the deepest hem), and mark the centre with a pin. With right sides upwards, place the sheet on a clean flat surface. Place the paper pattern strip under one half of this end of the sheet, placing it 10cm (4in) away from the hemmed edge with the flower heads facing the centre. Pin and carefully trace the three sets of gillyflower sprigs onto the fabric. Then repeat this process along the edge of the other half of the sheet but as a reversed tracing (see page 32).

4. Use an embroidery hoop to help keep the fabric flat and taut to prevent puckering. Use three strands of embroidery thread at all times.

5. Although the sprigs of gillyflower are repeated, their colouring can be different to encourage a more natural effect. Therefore, there is no definite colour plan to follow for this project. Use the illustration of the bed linen to help you choose how to use the different shades of green and pink, and keep a careful eye on the amount of each shade you are using so that you do not use the colours unevenly.

The darker shades of green are used for the lower ends of the stems, gradually working towards the flower, changing the shade from stem segment to segment. Use Stem Stitch widened into Satin Stitch to work all the stems and thin leaves, so that the stitches lie diagonally across the narrow shapes.

The flowers are all worked using two different shades of pink, one for the centre area and one for the jagged outer edges of the petals. You will see that some of them have deep pink centres, some do not and some only have speckles of the deeper shade around their centres.

To work the flowers, use a combination of Long and Short Stitch with Encroaching Straight Stitch. Fill in the flower petals with these stitches as if you were colouring them with crayons: make your stitches radiate from the centre to give the right effect.

6. To complete the embroidery, use the Yellow stranded thread to work four or five small curled Chain Stitch lines in the centre of each flower to represent the stamens.

7. When the stitchery is complete, press the sheet and pillowcase on the wrong side to remove creases and to encourage the stitchery to stand out with an embossed effect.

The combination of the slightly lustrous coton perlé thread and a careful selection of embroidery stitches produces a rich variety of textures to make these small designs so effective.

herb scented sachets

These pretty sachets are filled with herbs such as lavender or pot pourri and will gently fill the air with their perfume. They would make a very special gift whether given individually or as a pair. If you wish to make more, use the motifs given for the wildflower duvet cover (see page 112) and adapt the border pattern to suit whichever wildflower you have chosen.

materials to make two sachets

2 × 30cm (12in) squares of white evenweave fabric 11 threads per cm (27 threads per in) such as Zweigart

'Linda' E1235
40cm (16in) square of white cotton fabric
20cm (8in) square of pale pink cotton fabric
20cm (8in) square of pale mauve cotton fabric
1 skein each DMC Coton Perlé thread: Green 368, 369; Ecru; Mauve 554, 211; Pink 605, 899
2.75m (3yds) cream cotton lace edging, 2cm (¾in) wide
Cream or white sewing thread
Pink and mauve sewing thread to match fabric
Kapok or other filling

 Satin Stitch worked over five threads

 Satin Stitch worked over four threads

 Satin Stitch worked over two threads

 Lavender flowers of Bullion Stitch and Fly Stitch

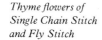 Thyme flowers of Single Chain Stitch and Fly Stitch

If you feel confident enough to work the leaves and flowers straight onto the fabric without marking their positions, trace only the shape of the plant onto the fabric. Then mark one corner to help you begin the border pattern.

Lavender
Pot pourri or some suitable herb
Suitable frame such as 23cm (9in) square frame
Green, mauve and pink crayons

to make the scented sachets

The two sachets have similar border patterns, with different central plant motifs so the same method is used for both sachets.

1. Carefully trace the stems, roots and main flowers on a sheet of tracing paper with a fine-tipped black felt pen. Also trace one corner of the border pattern (see green dotted line on trace-off pattern). Place this over a clean white surface and tape it in position. Then tape one piece of even-weave fabric over the tracing, lining up the straight grain of the fabric with the corner of the border.

2. Carefully trace the design on the fabric using sharp, appropriately coloured crayons. (If you cannot see the design clearly through the fabric, tape the tracing paper and fabric to a window and carefully trace the design.)

3. Stretch the fabric over the frame.
4. Work the centre motif.

thyme plant

Using Pale Green 369, work the main stems of the thyme plant in Stem Stitch. Where there are small side shoots, work them as single Straight Stitches. Where the stems join and become the thick 'trunk', work several lines of Stem Stitch side by side. Then, as this splits and divides to become the roots, return to separate lines of Stem Stitches, which then change into Back Stitches for the tips and ends.

Using the trace-off pattern as a guide, place the leaves along the stems. Form these small leaves by working two or three Straight Stitches next to each other, using Green 368. Grade their lengths gently to create very simple but effective leaf shapes.

You will see that the leaves are placed in pairs along the stems and then in groups of four at some of the stem tips. Also at the stem tips, work small Fly Stitches as indicated, to form the sepals of the flower buds. Then, using Deep Pink 899, work tiny Single Chain Stitches in the 'cup' of the Fly Stitches to represent the small buds. Add a few extra buds around the main flower clusters as indicated on the pattern guide. Similarly, work the open flowers in Pale Pink 605 as small clusters of two, three or four Single Chain Stitches to complete the thyme plant motif.

lavender plant

The stem, roots and leaves of the lavender plant are worked in the same way as the thyme plant. The leaves are worked much more freely than the thyme leaves by placing one or two Straight Stitches together for each leaf.

The flowers of the lavender plant are worked in Bullion Stitches, using one shade of Mauve 211 or 554 per stem and grouping several Bullion

Stitches around the stem in small clusters, pointing upwards and slightly outwards.

5. The border for each sachet has the same striped design on the outer and inner edges, which is worked by counting the threads of your fabric. Start counting at the corner that you have marked on the fabric and using Green 368 threads, work 103 Straight Stitches (over four threads) across the top of the herb motif, then down 103 stitches, across the bottom 103 stitches and finally up 103 stitches. (It is important that you follow the same pattern of working the corners, see below.)

Then work a narrow pale Green 369 border over two threads, followed by a wider Ecru border over five threads. Then leave a border of fifteen threads before working the outer bands of Green 368 and 369, and Ecru in the reverse order as before: Ecru over five threads, light Green 369 over two threads and darker Green 368 over four threads.

Finally, add the randomly arranged pattern in the centre of the border. The border for the thyme motif is formed by working small Fly Stitches in Green 368, scattering them in all directions, filling their 'cups' with tiny pale Pink 605 Single Chain Stitches.

The border for the lavender motif is formed by working slightly larger Fly Stitches in Green 368, spacing them apart so that you can then work a pale

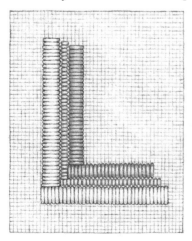

Draw the shape of the lavender plant and one corner onto the fabric.

Mauve 211 Bullion Stitch flower to fit into each 'cup'.

6. Remove the fabric from the frame and gently press it on the wrong side to remove any creases. Then trim the excess fabric, leaving a 1.5cm ($\frac{5}{8}$in) seam allowance all around the edge of the embroidered border.

Cut the lace edging equally and gather the two pieces; pin and baste it to the right side of each sachet face. Over this add the appropriately coloured fabric square. Machine around the sachet on the seam line, leaving a small gap.

Divide the white fabric into four 20cm (8in) squares and use to make two lining bags to fit the sachets. Place them inside the sachets, filling them with kapok and herbs. Use Slip Stitches to close the openings of the lining bags and the sachets.

Make a deep pink and deep mauve twisted cord (see page 135). Use four strands 2.5m (2$\frac{3}{4}$yd) in length for each cord. Tease the knotted ends to make tassels and sew the cords around the sachets, tying the ends in a neat bow in one corner.

Work the corners of the border lines of Satin Stitch like this.

43

the rose garden

The two canvaswork cushions are both worked from the same design. Reversing their background colours makes them look quite different.

Since medieval times, the rose has been cherished by gardeners and today it can be seen flourishing throughout the gardens of the world. Whether flowering only once each year with a strong, sweet scent, or producing brilliant and numerous blooms throughout the summer, the rose will provide an unforgettable display in any garden setting.

With modern methods of hybridization and cultivation, new varieties of roses appear each year, having been painstakingly grown to show new combinations and variations of colour, shape, scent and size. However, the old-fashioned rose, and indeed the wild or rambling types, still remain great favourites.

rose garden table set
(dog rose)

Instead of working the rose petals in solid stitchery, their outlines are clearly defined in Buttonhole Stitch. The tiny leaves are quickly and effectively worked in Fishbone Stitch.

The dog rose which has been the inspiration for this design is really a wild flower that can be seen today in hedgerows and scrubland, rather than in cultivated gardens. It is, however, the ancestor of the garden rose and has been well known for hundreds of years by the many and varied explanations of its name. One theory is that the ancient Greeks believed that its roots had special properties which would cure anyone bitten by a mad dog.

The pretty place mat and napkin set (see photograph on page 49) has been decorated with a border of entwined stems and clusters of flowers which are simply worked using only five stitches to give a rich, yet delicate effect.

materials for each place setting

45cm (18in) piece of pale pink cotton fabric 90cm (36in) wide, or readymade cotton napkin and place mat measuring 38cm (15in) square and 38 × 33cm (15 × 13in) respectively
Anchor stranded embroidery thread: 2 skeins each Pale Green 264; Light Green 254; Bright Green 255; Salmon Pink 11; Pale Pink 50; Bright Pink 54; 1 skein each Pale Orange 302; Pale Yellow 386
Pale green sewing thread (if making your own napkin and place mat)
20cm (8in) wooden embroidery hoop
Green and pink crayons

FOR SHORT SIDES OF OBLONG SHAPE OMIT LAST SET OF ▼ LEAVES + STEMS

to make the place setting

1. If you are going to make your own napkin and place mat, rather than use readymade ones, cut the fabric into two pieces: one measuring 45cm (18in) square for the napkin and the second measuring 45 × 40cm (18 × 16in) for the place mat.

Press each piece to remove any creases.

2. On tracing paper, draw a 33 × 27.5cm (13 × 10¾in) rectangle and a 33cm (13in) square. Fitting the border design into the corners of both shapes, carefully trace the entwined roses, using a black, fine-tipped felt pen. You will find that you have to omit a small section of stems and leaves, in order to fit the two shorter sides of the rectangle shape.

3. Place the completed designs on a flat surface with white paper underneath, so that the drawn lines show up well.

Then place your fabric over the appropriate design, centring it before fixing it temporarily to the flat surface with masking tape.

4. Using sharpened pink and green crayons, trace the design on the fabric. You need not trace the flower centres; they can easily be worked once the petals have been embroidered. Do not trace the dotted guide lines.

Omit the end leaves and stems of the long border when drawing the short sides of the rectangle for the place mat.

Fishbone Stitch is a quick and very effective way of making leaf shapes. Begin with a Straight Stitch at the leaf tip, then work down the leaf with closely positioned slanting stitches that overlap the centre line of the leaf shape.

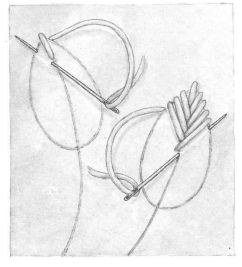

5. Place your fabric in the embroidery hoop to give a taut working area.

6. Use three strands of embroidery thread all the time.

Work the leaves and stems in the three shades of green, balancing the use of the colours evenly. The leaves are worked in Fishbone Stitch (see above), and the stems are worked in Stem Stitch.

The rose flowers are not filled in with solid stitchery, but are given their shape by outlines of closely worked Buttonhole Stitch. Use the three shades of pink randomly to work the flowers, but plan your colour sequence to ensure a balanced design.

Finally, work the flower centres.

Work tiny Pale Yellow 386 Straight Stitches radiating out from the centre of each flower. Work two tiny French Knots in the centre of this and then scatter more Knots on the ends of the Straight Stitches to represent the stamens. The French Knots may be worked in Pale Orange 0264, Pale Green 0254 or Light Green.

While working the embroidery, you will need to remove and reposition the embroidery hoop several times. Try to do this as few times as possible, as there is always a risk of marking your fabric.

7. Once the embroidery is complete, remove the hoop and press the fabric on the wrong side with a steam iron to encourage an embossed effect and to remove all creases.

8. Measure and lightly mark a 38cm (15in) square around the napkin border and 38 × 33cm (15 × 13in) rectangle around the place mat, making sure the designs are centred. Use the lines as a guide to work a decorative machine-stitched edge using the pale green sewing thread. Trim away the excess fabric. If your machine does not have this decorative facility, trim the excess fabric and work a tiny rolled hem.

rose scented sachet

This pretty sachet will gently perfume your bedroom as it hangs from its ribbons. The inspiration for this design is a dainty little rose called 'Baby Masquerade', which grows to no more than 38cm (15in) in height and has a mass of thimble-sized buds of pale orange which open out into a brilliant combination of yellow, pink and bright crimson petals. It is one of the floribunda group of roses, so it has a long and profuse flowering season. On each of the three sides of the sachet is a flower, fully opened and surrounded by several tiny buds, all linked by curving, twisting stems.

materials

30 × 50cm (12 × 20in) piece of pale pink cotton fabric
30 × 50cm (12 × 20in) piece of white backing fabric
Anchor stranded embroidery thread: 1 skein each Green 214, 254, 266; Yellow 302; Pink 9, 24, 36, 66, 892
Small amount of kapok or other filling
Pink sewing thread to match fabric
50cm (20in) Offray ribbon colour 240 'Persimmon', 6mm ($\frac{1}{4}$in) wide
Small sachet of rose-scented pot pourri
20cm (8in) wooden embroidery hoop or

The entwined pattern of stems, leaves and flowers of the dainty dog rose is used to create a very fresh and lively border design.

Space the three design motifs evenly on the fabric.

20 × 40cm (8 × 16in) rectangular frame
Pink and green crayons

to make the sachet

1. Press the pink and white fabric to remove any creases.

2. Transfer the design to a sheet of tracing paper and place it on a clean white surface. Place the pink fabric over the tracing, positioning it so that you can trace the design on it three times (see above).

Trace the design on the fabric using sharp-pointed crayons. Repeat this twice more to produce the three sides of the sachet.

3. If you are using a hoop, smooth the two layers of fabric together and baste across them so that they are held together. Position the fabric in the hoop, centring one of the design motifs in the middle of the hoop.

If you are using a rectangular frame, stretch the backing fabric and the pink fabric over the frame, ensuring that the grain of the fabric lies parallel to the sides of the frame.

4. Use three strands of thread at all times and work each side of the sachet in the same way.

Work the open rose flower in Buttonhole Stitch so that the bars of the stitches lie on the edge of each petal shape. Use the brightest shades of Pink 9 and 66 to work the outer petals, then the lighter shades 36 and 24, ending with the very pale Pink 892 around the centre. Fill the petal shapes evenly so that the backing fabric is completely covered with smooth stitching. The centre of the flower is worked in Yellow 302 French Knots to give a rich texture representing the stamens. Then, using the same Yellow thread, add small Straight Stitches at the innermost parts of the petals to give the characteristic brightness of the Baby Masquerade rose.

5. Next, work the leaves, stems and buds using the three shades of Green. You can arrange your own colours, but remember to balance the use of the three shades and avoid using one colour more than the others.

Work the stems of the rosebuds in small neat Stem Stitches. Then, when the stem thickens at the base of the bud, work Satin Stitch across the bulbous shape before working the sepals (small leafy parts which cover the bud) in Stem Stitch. Fill in the shape where necessary with a few Straight Stitches.

Work the stems of the leaves in small Back Stitches. Then work the leaves in Fishbone Stitch, beginning at the pointed tip of the leaf and then

CUTTING LINE MARK ON FABRIC

SEAM LINE DO NOT MARK ON FABRIC

Lightly draw the main design lines onto your fabric. The thorns and other small details can be freely stitched later.

working back towards the stem. Fishbone Stitch (page 48) is ideal for these tiny leaves and quite quick to work.

6. The thicker stems which curve and twist around each other are worked in Green 254 and 266 in double rows of Back Stitch to give a slightly thicker, more prominent line. Work them so that they will meet at the seams and appear to continue their curving shapes. (This is done by working Green 254 on the top stem as it appears from behind the lefthand side of the rose flower, and as the lower stem

When accurately worked, the design will appear as a continuous band around each side of the scented sachet.

Divide the ribbon equally into four pieces. Loop each piece and arrange at the top of the sachet and sew them securely in position.

on the righthand side.) Along the thicker stems, scatter tiny Straight Stitches to represent thorns. Use Pink 66 along the Green 266 stems, and Pink 9 along the Green 254 stems. Work the petals which are just emerging from the buds, using the two deepest shades of Pink 9 and 66; work tiny Buttonhole Stitches and then add highlights of Yellow 302 in Straight Stitch.

7. When you have embroidered the three faces of the sachet, carefully remove the fabric from the hoop or frame and press on the wrong side if there are any creases.

8. Cut out each piece along the marked cutting line. With right sides together, pin and baste two pieces along one side seam only. Make sure your seam coincides with the twisted stems of the design. Machine stitch in matching thread along the seam line (stitch only between the dots shown on the pattern) at the top and bottom of the shape.

9. Similarly, add the third embroidered piece with right sides together to the other two pieces, leaving a gap of 5cm (2in) along one seam. Extra care is needed at the points to ensure the seams converge in one place and do not overlap. If you have difficulty doing this on the sewing machine, a few neat hand stitches may be easier. Securely fasten off all the threads. Trim away a little of the seam allowance and very carefully snip it in towards the seam as this will help the seam to curve nicely on the right side.

10. Turn the sachet to the right side and smooth the curved seams into shape. Firmly stuff the sachet with kapok or other filling, adding the scented sachet in the centre of the filling.

Turn in the raw edges of the opening, and with matching thread make very small neat Slip Stitches to close the gap.

11. Divide the ribbon into four equal pieces. Loop and arrange them at one end of the sachet, and stitch them securely in position (see below).

r o s e   g a r d e n   c u s h i o n

The source of the design for this cushion is a rose called the Tall Scotch Rose. It has been cultivated since ancient times, and references have been found in the Herbals of Dodonaens and Gerard showing its existence in Europe since 1600.

The cushion is unusual in its execution. The centre spray is stitched in a free-style method, directly on the canvas. Around this area are four corner squares, each a stylized geometric design of rosebuds. To link the geometric corners and the free-style centre, basketweave stitchery is worked, providing an interesting contrast in textures.

By enlarging the background area of the centre and the corner panels, the total size could be enlarged to make a chair seat or stool top. Alternatively, this design could provide the theme for a set of cushions which could retain the same design, but vary in colour interpretation.

The stitches used for this canvaswork design are simple and quick to work: Basketweave Stitch, Tent Stitch, Straight Stitch and French Knots.

m a t e r i a l s

42cm (16in) square of canvas, 6 threads per cm (14 threads per in)
37cm (14½in) square of pale green linen-type fabric
Anchor Tapisserie yarn: 1 skein each Light Brown 0668; Light Champagne 0732; Deep Champagne 0702; 2 skeins each Mid Champagne 0366; Willow 0859; Pale Sage 3087; 9 skeins each Pale Green 3085; White 0402
35cm (14in) square cushion pad
Mid Champagne coloured sewing thread

p r e p a r a t i o n

Mount the canvas on the rectangular frame making sure that the canvas threads are parallel to the sides of the frame.

As the design incorporates two dif-ferent methods of transferring the design onto canvas, you will find it beneficial to count the threads of the canvas carefully and 'map out' where each section of the design will be worked.

t o   m a k e   t h e   r o s e g a r d e n   c u s h i o n

1. Count the threads as indicated on page 54, and mark the horizontal and vertical lines with a waterproof marker.

Following the direction of the stit-ches as shown on the chart (see page 57), work these lines in Tent Stitch using Light Brown 0668 and working over two vertical and two horizontal threads. These lines, once accurately established, will enable you to locate easily the remaining areas of the design.

2. Work the Basketweave or Weaving Stitch panels in Pale Green 3085, starting at the inner righthand corner of each centre side panel (see page 57).

3. Work the corner designs next. Work the squared stem shape in small Tent Stitch over one thread of canvas and then the buds and leaves in Straight Stitches, following the chart for the colour and direction of each stitch. Fill in the background with Tent Stitch.

4. Trace the central panel pattern (see page 55). Position the tracing under the canvas and draw the design lines on the canvas using a waterproof marker. Use Tent Stitch for the stems and Straight Stitch for the shaded petals and leaves.

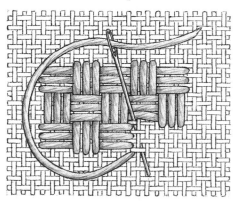

Basketweave or Weaving Stitch looks just as if the yarns are actually woven through each other giving the basket pattern. Work alternating blocks of three horizontal and three vertical Straight Stitches over four threads of canvas, tightly fitting the blocks closely side by side.

Count the threads of the canvas to find the position of the horizontal and vertical lines which divide the design into sections. Mark them with a waterproof pen and then embroider the lines in large Tent Stitch, working over two horizontal and two vertical threads.

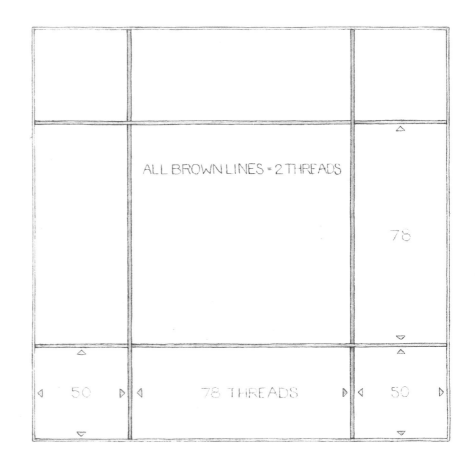

ALL BROWN LINES = 2 THREADS

78

△   △

◁   50   ▷ ◁   78 THREADS   ▷ ◁   50   ▷

▽   ▽

5. Work the leaves using the two deeper shades of Green 3087 and 0859 in Straight Stitch and their stems in Tent Stitch. The rosebuds are worked so that they echo the stylized buds of the corner designs, so adjust their positioning if necessary, so that they lie horizontally or vertically on the canvas. Use Light Brown 0668 for the outer edges of the buds, and fill in with Deep Champagne 0702.

6. The three full blooms are worked in close Straight Stitches. Begin each bloom with the Mid Champagne 0366 shade around the edges of the petals, blending in towards the centre using the Light Champagne 0732, and then the White 0402 yarn. Vary the Straight Stitches in length and angle them in towards the centre of the flower. Work Straight Stitches as though you were colouring the flowers with crayons on a piece of paper.

Work Light Brown 0668 French Knots in the centre of each flower for the pistil and surrounding stamens.

7. Complete the embroidery by filling in the centre background with small white Tent Stitches, working all the stitches in one direction.

8. Remove the canvaswork from the frame and trim the canvas to the same size as the pale green backing fabric. With right sides together, place the pieces together.

9. Pin, baste and then machine stitch around the cushion, working 1cm ($\frac{3}{8}$in) from the edge of the canvas, and leaving one side open. Clip across the corners and turn the cushion right side out. Insert the cushion pad and close the opening with invisible Slip Stitches.

10. Unwind the leftover skein of Mid Champagne 0366 yarn. Fold the length in half and use it to make a twisted cord (see Special Techniques, page 135).

11. Sew the twisted cord around the cushion on the seam line, twisting it to form a small loop at three corners and

Above, trace the motif onto the centre of the canvas. (Support the traced design on some books under the embroidery frame while doing this.)

The softly coloured Tall Scotch Rose has been effectively translated in the centre panel of the cushion, while in each corner there is a stylized pattern of rosebuds.

By carefully changing the colour scheme, you can produce a beautiful set of cushions with a common design theme.

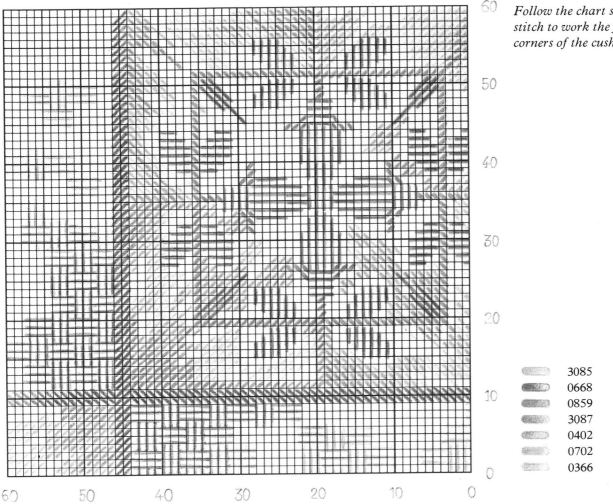

60
50
40
30
20
10
0

60   50   40   30   20   10   0

	3085
	0668
	0859
	3087
	0402
	0702
	0366

tying the ends in a neat bow at the fourth corner. Tie a knot at the ends of the cord before trimming the ends and then fluff out the cut ends of the yarn to make tassels.

alternative colour scheme

As you can see from the photograph, the design can be worked in variations of the same colour scheme to produce a beautiful set of cushions.

The alternative cushion has been worked by following the same stitch and design instructions, but changing some of the colours.

The Basketweave Stitch areas are worked in White 0402. The background Tent Stitch areas are worked in Pale Green 3085.

As the floral design is worked on a pale green background, the two shades of green used for the leaves and stems have to be slightly stronger and darker to make them stand out. So use Deep Willow 0215 instead of 0859, and Deep Sage 0281 instead of 3087.

When choosing the yarns for this colour scheme, remember to buy the correct amounts of the colours.

the spring flower garden

The simplicity of the tulip flower, with its long, graceful stem and curving leaves has inspired this fresh and crisp tray cloth.

S pring is the time of year that every gardener looks forward to, when the small shoots of winter strengthen and grow quickly in the brightening days, ready to burst into brilliant flowers and fresh, lush foliage.

Bulbs are always popular as they provide a beautiful display of colour, and many fill the air with heavy scents which are so welcome after the sparseness of the winter months.

Whether it is a large display of freely growing crocuses and daffodils across a lawn or a small cluster of perky tulips and hyacinths in a windowbox, the effect is the same: optimism for the summer to come.

grape hyacinth and snowdrop curtain tie-back

If you have plain curtains without a pattern or wish to pull your lace curtains away from the window, why not hold them in these pretty tie-backs?

The design is fresh and bright, showing snowdrops and grape hyacinths which are eagerly awaited in gardens in the early spring.

The instructions are given for one tie-back, which is ideal for a small window where the curtain is drawn to one side. If you wish to make more, simply multiply the amount of fabric and thread. (For some of the embroidery threads, you will need two skeins, but work the first tie-back to see how much thread you have left.)

The design would also look fresh and appealing if worked around a circular tablecloth and a small motif used to decorate matching napkins.

materials

50 × 60cm (20 × 24in) piece of pale blue cotton polyester
50 × 60cm (20 × 24in) piece of white cotton polyester
Anchor stranded embroidery thread: 1 skein each White; Blue 130, 131; Green 208, 211, 264, 267; Cream 386
Anchor Coton Perlé thread: 1 skein Green 242
2 small curtain rings
Sewing thread to match blue fabric and green Coton Perlé thread
Green and blue crayons
20cm (8in) wooden embroidery hoop
Tracing paper 60 × 25cm (24 × 10in)

to make the spring garden tie-back

1. Accurately draw the shape of the curtain tie-back (see page 62) by enlarging it using the grid method (see Special Techniques page 131). Then trace the flower motif (see page 61), reversing the tracing paper to draw the second half of it and match up the two sections. Place the motif centrally on the tie-back shape. Cut out the tie-back shape along the drawn line, which also represents the seam line.

2. Press the blue and white fabrics to remove any creases. Place the blue piece over the white, matching up the cut edges.

Measure and cut the layers of fabric into two pieces, each measuring 25 × 60cm (10 × 24in).

Reserve one set of pieces for the back of the tie-back.

3. With masking tape, secure the traced pattern over a clean white surface. Then tape the blue fabric over it, ensuring the pattern is positioned so that it fits within the fabric and allows 1cm ($\frac{3}{8}$in) all around for the seam allowance.

With pale green and blue crayons, accurately trace the design onto the fabric, keeping the drawn lines as fine as possible.

4. Remove the blue fabric and place it over the white backing fabric, aligning the edges and smoothing away any wrinkles. Baste the two layers to-

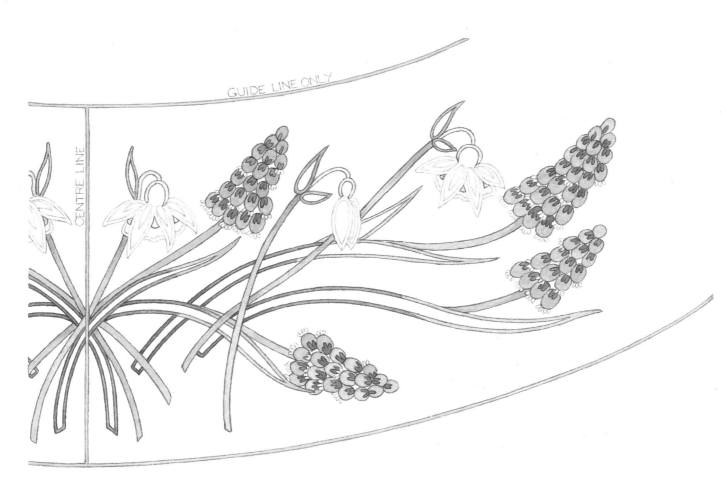

gether using Diagonal Basting Stitch to prevent them from moving away from one another during handling and when repositioning the embroidery hoop (see Special Techniques, page 134).

5. Place the fabric in the hoop, gently pulling the fabric to give a taut working area.

Use three strands of embroidery thread at all times.

6. As with several other designs in the book, the stitches in this project are used to give shape and texture as well as to help the onlooker understand the different parts of the design. Remember you are really 'drawing and colouring' your flowers with a needle and thread instead of a crayon.

The stitches used are predominantly a combination of Stem Stitch, Satin Stitch and Fishbone Stitch, which are all based on a simple single Straight Stitch, which is also used to make the tiny white frills

around some of the bell-like grape hyacinth flowers.

7. Starting with the snowdrops, work the gently curving stems in slanting Satin Stitches using Green 267. Work the small leafy shapes in the same shade in Fishbone Stitch, which is ideal for these small pointed shapes.

Then, using Green 264, work the small arched stalk in Stem Stitch, changing into Satin Stitch to build up the bulbous area of the flower.

The petals are worked in White using a mixture of Fishbone Stitch and Satin Stitch, filling each shape individually so that it retains its identity.

Then work a few Cream 386 Straight Stitches over the White stitches down the centre of each petal.

Using the trace-off pattern as a guide, work a few tiny Straight Stitches in Green 264 between each petal. Then in Cream 386, work very small

⬭	131
⬭	130
⬭	386
⬭	White
⬭	267
⬭	264
⬭	208
⬭	211

Trace the half section of the design onto paper. Then turn it over and, matching up the stems, carefully draw the second half to give the complete design.

The snowdrops and grape hyacinths on the tie-back have been realistically translated into stitchery by carefully selecting and using the most appropriate stitches.

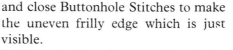

Accurately enlarge the half tie-back shape using the grid to help you. Repeat the enlarged shape to give the second half, joining it with the first along the centre line. Each square within the enlarged box must measure 52mm ($2\frac{1}{16}$in).

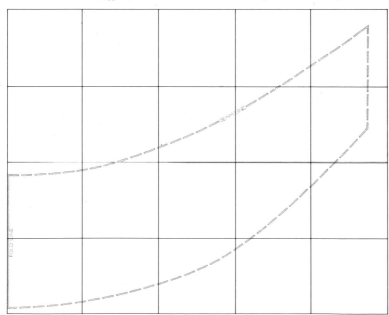

and close Buttonhole Stitches to make the uneven frilly edge which is just visible.

8. To embroider the grape hyacinths, use Green 208 to work the slanting Satin Stitch stems of the flowers. Then using the same shade, work the tips and upper parts of the leaves in Encroaching Straight Stitch, working the stitches so that they lie parallel to the sides of the long, thin leaves. Then gradually change the colour until you are working totally in the darker shade of Green 211 to fill the lower parts of the leaves.

Using Pale Blue 130, work the tiny oval shapes of the individual flowers in Satin Stitch. Then add two or three tiny Straight Stitches at the top of each flower, using the darker Blue 131. Shade the lower part of the top flowers.

To complete the embroidery, work three or four small white Straight Stitches pointing outwards from the base of the flowers. Do not add these white stitches to all the flowers, but only to the lower one or two rows and then randomly on a few other flowers to give a pleasing effect.

9. Remove all the basting threads and press the embroidered fabric on the wrong side to encourage an embossed effect to the stitchery. Place your traced pattern over the wrong side of the fabric, aligning the embroidery with the drawn design. With the pale blue crayon, draw accurately around the cut edge of the paper pattern to show the seam line.

Place the leftover white fabric on a flat surface, then place the blue piece over it, adding the embroidered layers with the right side facing downwards. Pin and baste the layers together around the seam line.

With blue sewing thread, machine stitch around the shape on the seam line, leaving a gap on the lower curved edge of approximately 10cm (4in).

Trim away the surplus fabric, leaving a narrow seam allowance and cutting across the corner points. Clip the allowance in towards the line of stitching.

Carefully turn to the right side and gently press to remove any creases.

Turn in the raw edges and hand stitch to close the opening.

10. Using the Coton Perlé thread, cover the curtain rings either by working Buttonhole Stitch over the ring or by using a small crochet hook to

cover it (see Special Techniques, page 136).
11. Use the remainder of the skein of Coton Perlé thread to make a twisted cord (see page 135).
12. Using two strands of Green 208,

hand sew the twisted cord around the edge of the tie-back, neatly concealing the ends of the cord at one corner.

Hand stitch the curtain rings in the middle of the short sides of the tie-back with matching thread.

Overleaf, accurately match up the four quarters of the design so that the tulip stems and leaves join and flow into one another.

t u l i p   t r a y   c l o t h

The bold design of this tray cloth has been worked entirely in Buttonhole Stitch to give a firm and secure edge to all the worked shapes. The technique used is known as cutwork, as small areas are cut away, leaving 'holes' in the design which look very effective against the solid areas of fabric as seen in this example.

Fabric crayons have been used with great effect to give soft colouring to the fleshy leaves, stems and flowers of the tulips, which contrasts and complements the neat lines of stitchery.

m a t e r i a l s

50 × 60cm (20 × 24in) piece of white polyester mix linen-type fabric
DMC stranded embroidery thread:
2 skeins Green 562, 563; 1 skein Green 955, 989; small amounts Yellow 745, 972; Pink 776, 899
1 packet fabric transfer crayons (Crayola)
38 × 50cm (15 × 20in) sheet of tracing paper
20cm (8in) wooden embroidery hoop

to make the tray cloth

1. Make your transfer pattern. Without folding, find the centre guide lines of the length and width of the tracing paper. (Do not fold the paper; if you draw over the fold with the fabric crayons, the fold line will show up and appear as a stronger colour when transferred onto the fabric.) Mark the lines with a ruler and fine-tipped felt pen.

Align the quarter section of the design under one quarter of your paper so that the dotted lines of the design match up with your centre guidelines

on the paper. Carefully draw the tulip design on the paper using a felt pen. Turn the paper around, and align the next quarter section of the paper over the design so that it joins up with the first quarter. Repeat this process twice more so that you complete the tray cloth design.

Make a small test strip using the fabric crayons on a spare piece of the fabric in order to see the strength of the colours. For this project you want to achieve soft and subtle shades of green and pink with a tinge of orange.

Carefully colour in the stems, leaves and petals of the tulips, pressing gently with the crayons and remembering to make the strokes of the crayon marks lie along the length of the shapes to give

The soft pinks and greens of the tulips have been achieved effectively by using fabric transfer crayons.

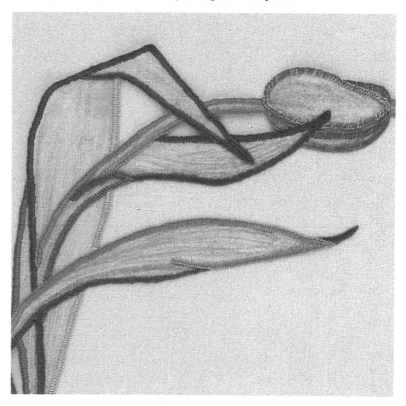

CUT AREAS

the visual impression of growth of the plants.

Read the manufacturer's instructions carefully before transferring the crayonned design to the centre of the crease-free fabric. Remember not to move the paper while transferring the design as this will cause a smudged and blurred effect.

2. Place one area of your design in the embroidery hoop, pulling the fabric around the hoop gently to achieve a taut working area.

Use three strands of thread at all times and work small neat lines of closely spaced Buttonhole Stitches around all the design areas. Work the Buttonhole Stitches so that the bars of the stitches lie on the outer edge of the design edge (see right).

To embroider the tulip flowers, use two strands of Pink 776 and one of Yellow 745 grouped together to give a streaked effect of the inner petal lines,

and then two strands of Pink 899 and one of Yellow 972 around the outer petal lines.

Then use the different shades of green to work the leaf and stem lines, using the shades 562 and 563 more than the other two shades. The positioning of the different green shades does not have to be symmetrical, but it must look balanced.

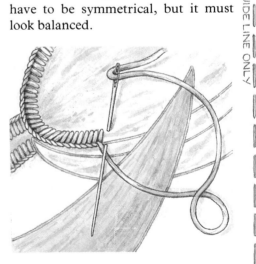

3. When you have completed all the stitchery, press the fabric firmly on the wrong side to remove all creases. Use a spray starch to give a slightly stiff effect, which will not only make the tray cloth look much nicer, but will also make it easier for you to cut away the small holes in the design.

4. With a pair of small, sharp-pointed scissors, *very carefully* cut away the small areas that have been formed by the leaves, stems and flowers overlapping in the design (see the grey areas on the trace-off pattern) and then cut away the excess fabric around the edges of the tray cloth. Press the tray cloth once more. Spray starch may be used at this stage if you wish.

Your Buttonhole Stitches must be closely spaced and very evenly worked to create the desired effect (see detail opposite).

Below left, it is much easier to trace the design onto the fabric if it is stretched within the hoop; then place the hoop upside down over the design so that the fabric lies flush on top of it.

Below right, you do not need to trace every tiny detail onto your fabric, just the main shapes of the designs.

Overleaf, spring flowers are always so popular that the sight of them on the tie-back or gift cards will surely give pleasure at any time of year.

h y a c i n t h   a n d   c r o c u s   g i f t   c a r d s

With a little time and only a small amount of fabric and yarn, you can make these delightful gift cards.

A handmade card always says much more than one that has been mass-produced, and these cards can be mounted and framed as permanent keepsakes by the recipient.

materials

25cm (10in) square of white fabric

1 oval 8 × 10cm (3 × 4in) frame greetings card

1 circle 8cm (3in) diameter frame greetings card

Small amounts of Anchor stranded embroidery thread: Brick 336, 337; Blue 128, 129; Yellow 303, 311; Mauve 95; Green 214, 266, 860; Brown 393

Adhesive glue suitable for fabric and card

20cm (8in) wooden embroidery hoop

to make the spring garden gift cards

1. Press the fabric to remove any creases. Place it in the embroidery hoop, pulling the fabric around the outside gently to give a taut working area.

2. Place the hoop flat down (see below left) over the tracing of the hyacinth design, positioning the design in one half of the hoop. Carefully and accurately draw the design onto the

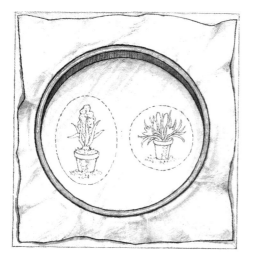

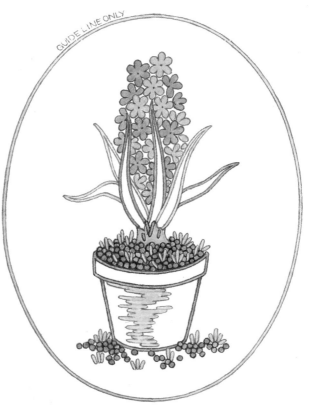

GUIDE LINE ONLY

fabric using appropriately coloured pencils. Then reposition the hoop over the crocus design and draw this onto the fabric. Leave at least 3cm (1¼in) between the two motifs and lightly draw the dotted lines of the circle and the oval.

If you prefer to work with the fabric uppermost on the hoop, remove it and reposition it in the hoop.

3. Use three strands of thread at all times.

Use Brick 337, work Back Stitches around the flowerpots on the design lines. Then work Satin Stitch around the rim of the pot, working the stitches vertically so that they go over the Back Stitches to give a slightly raised effect. Then work Long and Short Stitches around the main part of the pot, working the stitches so that they lie around the pot in contrast to the short vertical stitches on the rim. Try to curve your stitches to give the rounded shape of the flowerpot. To emphasize this, add highlighting to the pot by using Brick 336 to work an irregular 'stripe' of the lighter shade down the pot (see illustration for detail).

Work the soil, using Brown 393 to build up a solid area of tiny French Knots within the top of the pot, and then scatter clusters of Knots at the base of the pot as if the soil has spilled out onto the ground around the pot. Make each Knot small by winding the thread just once around the needle. Add a few tiny Straight Stitches using Green 266 to represent small shoots appearing through the soil.

Work the foliage of both the crocus and the hyacinth plants in a combination of Green 214 and 860. Work lines of Stem Stitch close together for the crocus leaves, and use a combination of Long and Short Stitch and Split Stitch to make the fleshy leaves of the hyacinth. Add a few Straight Stitches at the base of the hyacinth leaves in

The crocus trace-off

Brick 336 and Brown 393 to represent the tip of the bulb.

Work the flowers of the hyacinth in groups of Single Chain Stitch using Blue 128 and 129, merging the colours and building up the richness of the individual flowers into the mass of colour that is so typical of the hyacinth plant.

Then work the crocus flowers in Satin Stitch, changing to Stem Stitch where the shapes become narrow, using Yellow 303 and 311. Then add a few Straight Stitches using Mauve 95 to give the delicate mixture of colour that is sometimes seen in crocus flowers.

4. When you have completed the embroidery, remove the fabric from the hoop and press it firmly on the wrong side to remove any creases and to make the stitchery stand out on the right side. Trim the excess fabric away around the motifs, leaving at least 1.5cm (⅝in) around the dotted lines.

5. Carefully place each embroidered motif behind the 'frame' of the greetings cards, using a little clear adhesive glue to hold them securely in position.

The finely worked gift cards show the rich textures and patterns that are created when the embroidery thread is used to form different stitches.

town gardens

The tie-back is worked from a chart, while the cushion is more freely created by drawing the outlines on canvas and then 'filling' them in.

*t*o the majority of town and city dwellers, a garden is a haven and a breath of fresh air among the greyness of concrete and the angular world of walls, roofs and buildings.

Whether it is a tiny walled yard or a larger grassy patch, the town garden can benefit from its urban environment, as it will be more sheltered and therefore warmer in the winter than its country cousin and will allow otherwise difficult plants to survive and flourish.

With space at a premium in towns and cities, every inch is put to good use by the gardening enthusiast, from the window ledge and doorstep to the shaded corner; all can be the home of some plant or other.

A narrow patio or even a small roof terrace can be completely transformed by a careful arrangement of textures and colours provided by different types of ground cover, whether plant or paving stone. One of the nice points to consider when gardening in a town is the fact that space is usually very limited. This in turn requires only small numbers of plants, which can be looked after relatively easily and at low cost, but with great effect, producing a colourful display throughout the seasons.

curtain tie-back

Many gardens in towns and cities are extremely limited in size, yet whatever their dimensions they can with careful planning be transformed into areas of beauty.

This subtly-coloured canvas-work tie-back shows rows of stylized plants, separated by the simple pattern of a paved footpath, which could so easily be all the town gardener has to work with.

The neat pattern of paving stones along a terrace is emphasized by the alternating direction of the coton perlé stitches which subtly catch the light.

materials

15 × 60cm (6 × 24in) petit point canvas
7 threads per cm (17 threads per in)
DMC Coton Perlé thread No. 5: 2 skeins each Cream 712; Fawn 842; 1 skein Yellow 743
DMC soft embroidery cotton: 2 skeins each Green 2369, 2564; 1 skein each Blue 2800, 2798; Salmon 2758, 2357
12 × 51cm (4¾ × 20in) backing fabric of your choice
Sewing thread to match
2 small curtain rings
30cm (12in) tapestry frame (rotating type)
Small crochet hook

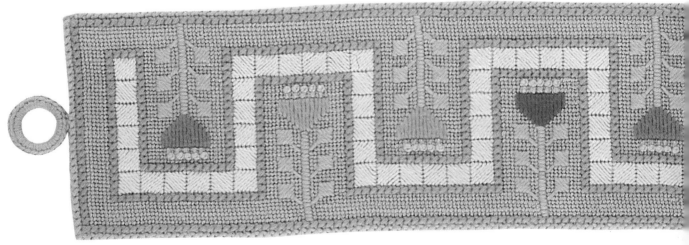

to make the tie-back

1. Mount the short ends of the canvas on the rotating sides of the frame and roll the canvas around one of these sides.

Using the rotating frame enables you to roll and unroll the canvas so that you can work backwards and forwards along the narrow strip of canvas quite easily within a convenient size of frame.

2. With Cream Coton Perlé and referring to the chart on page 72 and the photograph below, begin by stitching the footpath in a variation of Square Mosaic Stitch to produce the effect of paving stones; the lustre of the Perlé thread worked in different directions catches the light in a pleasing way.

3. Once you have worked the paving stones, work the border of Green Cross Stitch on each side of the path (make all the top stitches of the Cross Stitches face the same direction).

4. Following the chart (see overleaf) carefully, position the plants within each space formed by the pattern of the path. Work the main stem of each plant before working the diagonal side stems. These side stems are single Straight Stitches worked from the main stem upwards and outwards to the tip of

each leaf. The leaf is then worked over the side stem.

Once you have worked the stems and leaves of each plant, work the flower heads, alternating the light and dark shades of Blue 2800 and 2798 along one side of the path and similarly the two shades of Salmon 2758 and 2357 along the other side.

Do not work the yellow stamens at this stage.

5. Work the background in Fawn 842 in Tent Stitch to fill in all the surrounding areas, ensuring that all the stitches face the same direction.

6. Then work the outer border in the two shades of Green 2369 and 2564, using Cross Stitch and remembering to make the stitches face the same way as those Cross Stitches around the footpath.

7. Finally, work the stamens in Yellow 743, spacing five of them evenly along the top of each flower head. Work small Straight Stitches (over two threads of canvas and on top of the Fawn Tent Stitch background). Then work a French Knot at the end of each stitch.

8. Remove the canvas from the frame and trim away the excess, leaving a 1cm ($\frac{3}{8}$in) seam allowance on all sides.

Then with right sides together, pin and baste the backing fabric and the canvas together. With the canvas

Overleaf, carefully follow the tie-back chart, stitch by stitch.

	2564
	2369
	842
	2800
	712
	2357
	743

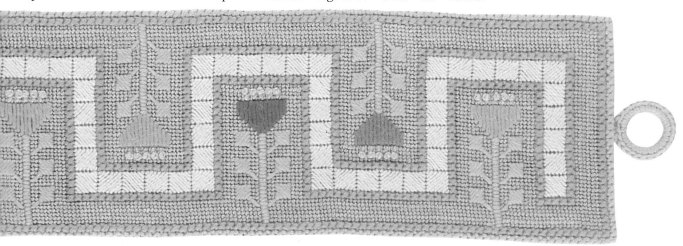

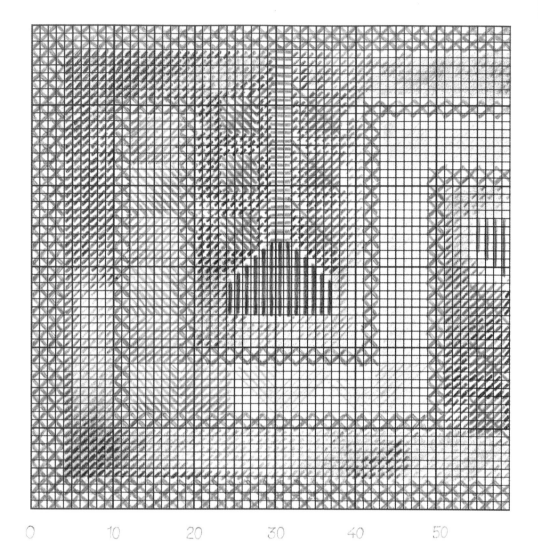

0   10   20   30   40   50

Tent Stitch worked over one vertical and horizontal thread

Cross Stitch worked over two vertical and horizontal threads forming tie-back border

Squares of Straight Stitch worked diagonally across the canvas alternating in direction

facing upward, machine stitch along the edge of the stitchery, leaving a gap on one of the longer sides of approximately 10cm (4in). Clip across the corners and carefully turn the tie-back to the right side.

Fold in and hand stitch the two edges of the opening together.

Using the small crochet hook, cover the two curtain rings with Green 2564 (see Special Techniques, page 136) and carefully hand stitch one in the centre of each short end of the tie-back with matching thread.

town garden canvaswork cushion

This richly worked cushion has as its theme the geometric patterns of rows of gardens and vegetable patches often seen on the edges of a town. The naive aerial view looks down on the gardens while the house fronts face upwards.

The design is worked in a mixture of traditional canvaswork with additional surface stitchery to give an extra textural quality. Also a combination of tapestry yarns and soft embroidery threads is used to give a subtle variety.

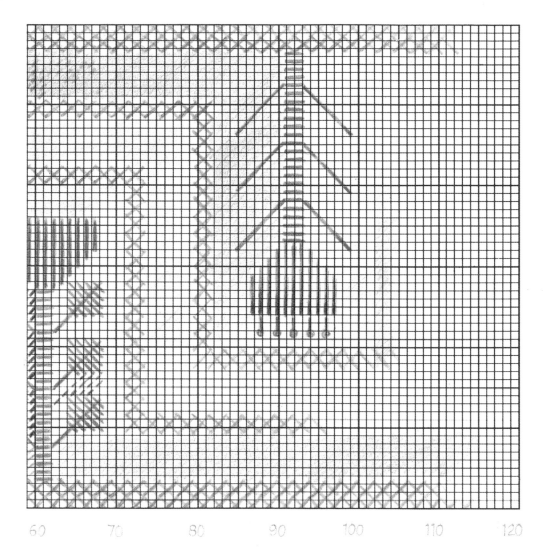

60   70   80   90   100   110   120

m a t e r i a l s

*50cm (20in) square of mono canvas 6
holes per cm (14 holes per in)*
*DMC tapestry yarn: 4 skeins Light
Brown 7500; 3 skeins each Green
7370, 7364, 7393, 7400; 2 skeins
each Light Brown 7543, 7143, 7144;
Green 7382*
*DMC soft embroidery cotton: 5 skeins
Brown 2405; 3 skeins Blue-grey
2932; 1 skein each Salmon 2357;
Pink 2572; Dark Grey 2241; Light
Grey 2415; Light Green 2472; Dark
Green 2320*
*35cm (14in) square of grey cotton
backing fabric*
33cm (13in) square cushion pad
Grey sewing thread

*40cm (16in) square wooden frame or
similar*
*Waterproof or permanent marking pen
suitable for marking canvas*
Tracing paper

t o   m a k e   t h e   t o w n
g a r d e n   c u s h i o n

1. Using a large sheet of tracing paper,
carefully and accurately draw the
entire design using the quarter trace-
off pattern provided, repeating the
quarter section and matching up the
design to form the complete cushion.
You may find it easier to make four
photocopies of the quarter design, trim
along the dotted lines and then carefully
join the four pieces together.

 *Straight Stitch over
two Tent Stitches with
French Knots on top*

*Straight Stitch
flowers, stitches of
different lengths*

*Straight Stitch stems
and leaves, in different
lengths and directions*

*Reversed Sloping
Gobelin Stitch fence in
four colours*

 Satin Stitch house walls

 *Tent Stitch soil in
flowerbeds and
vegetable patches*

 Tent Stitch doors

 *French Knot hedges in
three colours*

 *Satin Stitch grass
strips*

 *Satin Stitch grass
strips*

 *Diagonal Satin Stitch
outer edge of design*

 *Tent Stitch window
frames*

 *Diagonal Satin Stitch
roofs*

 *Tent Stitch glass in
windows*

 *Tent Stitch tops of
fences in four colours*

*Previous page, whether
the idea has come from
the Vegetable Garden,
the Town Garden or the
Formal Garden, the
result is the same, a
delightful design full of
colour and texture.*

2. With masking tape, secure the completed design to a flat, white surface and then place the piece of canvas centrally on top, aligning the threads of the canvas with the horizontal and vertical lines of the design pattern.

3. Using the waterproof marking pen, carefully trace the design lines on the canvas.

4. Stretch the canvas on the wooden frame. Make sure the threads of the canvas are parallel to the sides of the frame to prevent the possibility of distortion taking place during working.

5. You are now ready to begin stitchery.

With this method of canvaswork, you are working to a design drawn onto the canvas. You are not counting the stitches and following a chart, therefore the shapes such as the windows or flowerbeds may not all be identical. This need not detract from the beauty of the design, but will add to the charm of this childlike view of a townscape.

6. Using Brown 2405, work Tent Stitch in the central section (it does not matter which way the stitches lie as long as they are all the same).

7. Using Green 7370, 7364 and 7393, work French Knots around the central flowerbed. Work the three colours randomly to give a speckled effect, and keep your stitches close together to produce a richly textured hedge.

8. Around the hedge work a line of Satin Sitches, using Green 7400 to represent a grassy border. Then around this, work a Tent Stitch border in Blue-grey 2932. This gives you the centre of the design around which the houses, gardens and vegetable patches are made.

9. Using Blue-grey 2932, work the window frames in Tent Stitch. Try to keep all the windows the same size. Then using the same colour, work the roofs in Diagonal or Oblique Satin Stitches.

Using Light Grey 2415, work a line of Tent Stitch along the base of each roof.

Fill in the windows with Dark Grey

2241, using Tent Stitch to face the same direction as the stitches of the window frames.

Then, with Green 7370, 7364 and 7393, work the three doors of each row of houses in Tent Stitch, using one shade of green per door. Repeat the same colour sequence on each row of houses.

The house walls are worked in Light Brown 7500 in horizontal and vertical rows of Satin Stitches (repeat the way you fill in the walls of the first row when working the other three rows of houses).

10. Using Light Brown 7543, 7500, 7143 and 7144, work randomly shaded rows of Tent Stitch to represent the tops of the fences that divide the gardens and vegetable patches.

11. Using Green 7400, work lines of Satin Stitches around the vegetable patches in each corner of the design. Similarly, use Green 7382 to work rows of Satin Stitches side by side to form the lawns of the gardens (divide each lawn evenly into three to work the Satin Stitch rows).

12. Then fill the vegetable patches and the flowerbeds around the lawns with Brown 2405, working the Tent Stitches so that along each side they lie in the same direction.

13. Around the gardens and vegetable patches, work the hedge border to match the centre hedge.

14. The fence is worked in Light Brown 7543, 7500, 7143 and 7144 in Reversed Sloping Gobelin Stitch (see page 79). Use one shade per 'strip of fence', using the four shades randomly along each side of the design.

15. Work a border of Diagonal (Oblique) Satin Stitch around the fence, using Light Grey 2415, and then in the same stitch, work another border in Blue-grey 2932.

You have now covered the canvas and are ready to work the surface stitchery details of the flowers and vegetables.

16. Using Dark Green 2320, work small Straight Stitch plants in the

*Draw the main design
lines of the trace-off
pattern onto your
canvas, then refer to the
pattern to work the
details of the design.*

CENTRE

This naively simple view
of a town has a central
square surrounded by
rows of houses and tiny
gardens, while in the
corners are orderly
vegetable patches.

centre flowerbed. Work French Knot flowers on each plant, using Pink 2572 and Salmon 2357 (see middle right).

17. Then using Light Green 2472, work similar plants along the sills of the upper windows of the end houses of each row with pink French Knot flowers and on the sill of the middle ground floor window with salmon flowers.

18. Using Green 2320, work these same plants evenly around the garden lawns, with salmon flowers around the small square lawns and pink flowers around the oblong lawns on each side.

19. Finally, work the vegetables, using Light Green 2472 to form tiny cabbages in the centre patch by working clusters of French Knots. Then in the corner patches, work two lines of evenly spaced Single Knot Stitches, using double thread. Trim the threads to give short fluffy tufts. Then in the remaining vegetable patch, work randomly placed Single Knot Stitches, using only a single thread. Trim the threads to give short tufts (see immediately right). You may wish to practise this stitch before working it on the canvas.

20. Your canvaswork cushion top is now complete.

Remove it from the frame and trim away the excess canvas, leaving a 1.5cm ($\frac{5}{8}$in) seam allowance all around the stitchery.

Place the canvaswork downwards on the grey backing fabric. Pin, baste and machine stitch the layers together using matching grey sewing thread. Leave a gap of at least 20cm (8in) along one side.

Trim the excess seam allowance and clip the corners close to the line of stitching before turning to the right side.

Place the cushion pad inside the cover and then turn in the raw edges of the opening. With grey sewing thread, close the opening using tiny Slip Stitches.

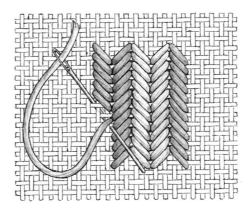

Reversed Sloping Gobelin Stitch is used to represent the garden fences. Work each individual stitch over two vertical and horizontal threads.

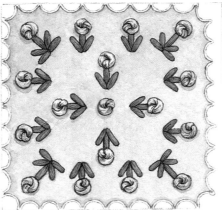

Three Straight Stitches for the leaves and stem with a French Knot flower make each plant in the central square.

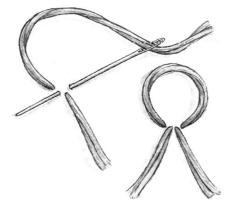

Single Knot Stitch: pass the needle to the back of the fabric and bring it out to the left and up a little. Leave a short tail of thread hanging. Insert the needle to the right of the tail, bringing it out close to, but on the left of the tail. Pull the yarn tightly and cut the thread.

the
vegetable
garden

The rich textures and colours within the vegetable
garden are as inspiring as any floral display.

*t*he vegetable garden might not spring to mind if you were asked to list the different kinds of garden, but it is probably one of the oldest types, and certainly one of the most satisfying. Indeed, many people would keenly argue that a well-tended vegetable garden is as attractive a sight as a flower garden, with its rows of lush vegetation, whether it is the feathery fern-like carrot tops or the heavy growth of the cabbage.

To plan, sow and maintain a vegetable garden each year is a time-consuming pursuit, but the end product is always a great reward at harvest time.

the vegetable sampler

In this project, the idea of neatly ordered rows of vegetables, whether growing or gathered, is used in conjunction with the style of the old-fashioned sampler. However, the method of work is quite different from that of a sampler where Cross Stitch is the most usual way of interpreting the design. Here, richly worked areas of solid stitchery can be seen, and some interesting Stumpwork techniques have been used to give the free-standing and three-dimensional effect of the stalks of the radishes and tomatoes.

To enhance the richness of the stitchery, Coton Perlé thread has been used. This lustrous thread is ideal when used to build up a design such as this one.

materials

45 × 60cm (18 × 24in) piece of white linen-type fabric such as Zweigart 'Linda' No. E1235
45 × 60cm (18 × 24in) piece of white cotton backing fabric
DMC Coton Perlé No. 5 thread: 2 skeins each Green 954, 704; 1 skein each Green 906, 369; Yellow 3078, 745; Mauve 601, 604; Red 900, 349
Small scraps of heavyweight interfacing (pelmet weight)
2m (2yd) thin string
30 × 43cm (12 × 17in) firm cardboard
Strong button thread
36 × 50cm (14 × 20in) oblong wooden frame (approximate size)
Fabric transfer pencil
Tracing paper

to make the sampler

1. Using the trace-off pattern, make your own paper transfer using the special pencil (follow the manufacturer's instructions). You will need a piece of tracing paper (or greaseproof paper) 30 × 43cm (12 × 17in). Draw your border outline as a tiny dotted line very lightly so that it will not show when stitched, as this area is not solidly covered. You need eight strips in which the vegetables are placed. If you look at the illustration of the finished sampler, you can see that the vegetables are arranged in a repeat pattern, but that the second row of each group is reversed to create a more interesting design. You can follow this idea by simply taking a tracing of the vegetables and then turning the paper over and working from this side for the second row of each vegetable.

Alternatively, you may wish to have all the lines the same and simply rearrange the sequence of repeats.
2. Stretch the white cotton backing fabric over the oblong frame, ensuring that the grain of the fabric is parallel to the sides of the frame. Similarly, stretch the linen-type fabric on the frame.

Place a pad of spare fabric on a smooth surface and place the transfer face upwards on top. Then put the frame down centrally onto the transfer so that the fabric is resting on the paper. Following the manufacturer's instructions, carefully transfer the design to the fabric.
3. You are now ready to begin the stitchery.

Start by working the tiny border pattern, using Green 704. The lines are small, irregularly worked Straight Stitches which give the impression of blades of grass. (They are spaced apart, but must be close enough together to hide the transfer marks on the fabric.)

4. The rows of radishes are worked in a combination of stitches to give the solid shapes of the radish roots.

Work the radishes predominantly in Mauve 601, changing to Mauve 604 as the root becomes thin and twisted.

Work a line of Back Stitch around the edge of the rounded part of the radish root, and then work over this, placing your stitches carefully so that they encourage the rounded effect. Use a mixture of Long and Short Stitch and Encroaching Straight Stitch to build up the solid area.

You will find that the two stitches merge and you will be more concerned with filling in and building up the shape rather than working lines of any particular stitches.

It is easier if you work the deep

To make the stalks, work two or three Straight Stitches from the radish top, meeting at a point to give the 'bars' on which the needleweaving is worked. Bring the needle out close to the radish edge and begin weaving in and out of the bars. Continue weaving backwards and forwards until the bars are completely hidden. Then take the needle down through the fabric at the point and bring it out ready to work the 'bars' for the next stalk.

1.

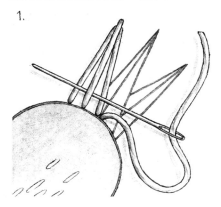

2.

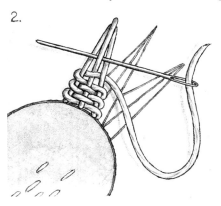

1.

2

3.

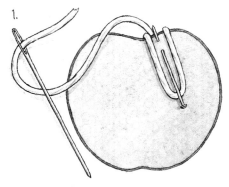

4.

Picots are worked where the stalks hang freely. To work a picot, make a loop on the top of the fabric. Then insert a pin over the loop and into the fabric. Pass the threaded needle behind the pin and then weave it backwards and forwards through the threads until they are filled. Pass the needle down through the fabric, bringing it up again in position for the next picot.

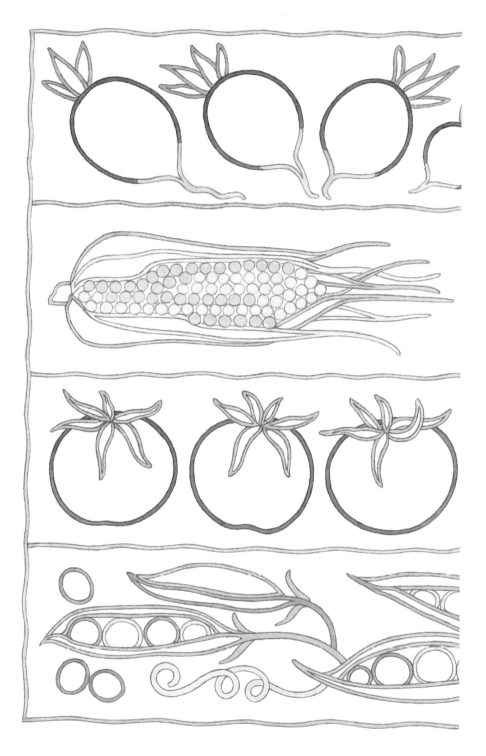

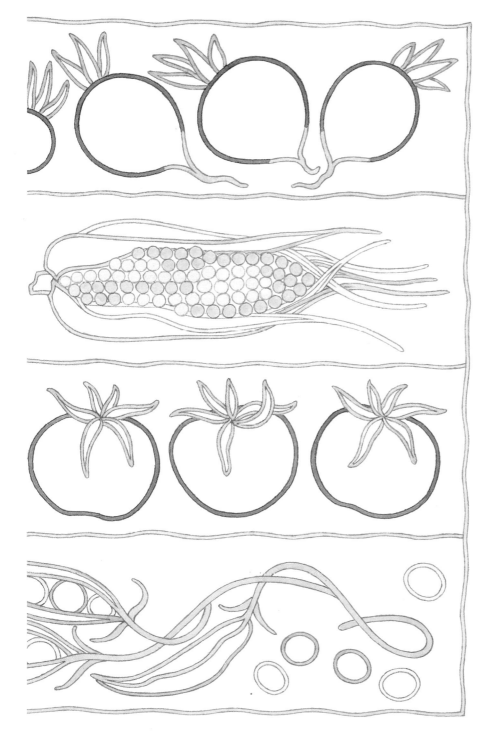

Trace each row of vegetables twice in this order or reverse them, or even rearrange the sequence.

mauve area first. Then the pale mauve can be used to finish off each shape by working a few tiny Straight Stitches on top of the deep mauve to give a slightly speckled effect.

Then the thin twisted root end is easily worked by changing the stitches into Stem Stitches.

Try to vary the shading of the two mauve colours on each radish, and remember, if you do not feel satisfied with a particular area, you can carefully remove the wrongly placed stitches and rework them.

The radish stalks are worked by needleweaving, a type of Stumpwork (which means that the stitches are raised above the level of the fabric) to give the realistic leafy stalk shapes. Work three or four of these at the top of each radish (see page 83).

5. The rows of corn-on-the-cob (maize) are also worked using a mixture of Long and Short Stitch and Encroaching Straight Stitch, to build up the leafy outer cases of the cobs, while the corn pieces are represented by a mass of French Knots to make a very textured area. Use Green 704 and 369 to work the leafy areas, picking out the shapes of the individual leaf shapes by placing the lighter green next to the deeper green and planning where the colours will go. Remember, each corn-on-the-cob should be slightly different to give an interesting effect.

The stitches are worked so that they lie along the length of each cob to give shape to the leaves. This also allows you to taper them into points by working the last few stitches of each leaf in Stem Stitch. Work the corn pieces using the two shades of Yellow 3078 and 745. You will find it more effective if you work the French Knots in lines along the cob rather than across it, varying from one shade of yellow to the other. If you wish, you can work with two needles threaded with the two shades and use them simultaneously.

To achieve a large, rounded knot,

wind the thread around the needle three times when making each stitch.

6. The rows of tomatoes are worked in a similar way to the radishes. The bright red fruits are worked in Long and Short Stitch and Encroaching Straight Stitch to give the rounded, solid shapes. Use the two shades of Red 900 and 349, merging the two together as suggested on the trace-off pattern, varying them as you work.

The tomato stalks are worked in Green 906, in a slightly different way to those of the radishes, as they are partly worked by the needleweaving method (see page 83), but also by using another Stumpwork technique which makes tiny, hanging leaf shapes called 'picots'. If you look closely at the illustration of the vegetable sampler, you will see that the leafy parts of the stalk which lay over the tomato shape are these hanging picots. The others, which have their tips on the white background fabric, are made by the needleweaving method. Try to make the bars loosely so that they are slightly longer than the distance they have to cover. Then when the thread has been woven in and out to build up the leaf, the shape will twist and curve in a pleasing way. You can even work them over and under one another.

Work the picot stalks of the tomatoes following the steps on p. 83.

Try to vary the stalks from one tomato to another. Most of them will have four parts made by needle-weaving and two by making picots. Once they are all worked, twist them a little to make them look more interesting.

7. Work the row of peas and pods using the three shades of Green 954, 704 and 369, referring to the illustration of the sampler to help you.

Thread the thin string into a large needle and couch this down along the lines of the stems, covering it completely to give a very raised and rounded effect. It is better to work the Couching Stitches at an angle across

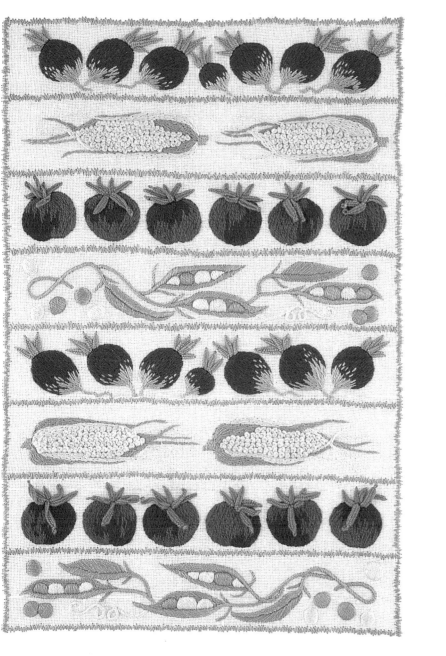

The rich versatility of coton perlé thread is exploited in the sampler. With the use of subtle padding and simple stumpwork techniques, a striking three-dimensional effect is achieved.

the string rather than at right angles. Where the stem turns into a pod, continue the string up to the point of the pod and then take it through to the wrong side. Then cover the string with longer Satin Stitches to fill the pod area as well. Work the other side of the pod in the same way, but do not use the string; slant the stitches towards the pod's tip.

The peas are made to look rounded and full by placing a small round pad of carefully cut-out interfacing in po-sition and then working Satin Stitches closely and evenly over the pad.

Remember to vary the use of the three shades of green thread.

8. Once you have worked all the rows of vegetables, carefully remove the fabric from the frame. Trim away a little of the fabric and then lace it tightly over the cardboard, using the button thread.

9. Place your vegetable sampler in a carefully chosen frame. Remember not to use glass as you do not want to flatten the stitchery.

carrots and mushrooms

These two eyecatching pictures will enhance your kitchen or brighten up the dining area with their strong colours and shapes. The heavily stitched vegetables appear quite solid and three-dimensional, while around them are simply stylized versions of the same vegetables.

The use of Stumpwork 'picots', which have also been used on the Vegetable Sampler (page 82), bring the carrot stalks to life and make it difficult for the onlooker not to want to touch and rearrange them.

carrot picture

materials

40 × 50cm (16 × 20in) piece of white evenweave linen-type fabric such as Zweigart 'Linda' No. E1235
40 × 50cm (16 × 20in) piece of white cotton backing fabric
1 skein each DMC No. 5 Coton Perlé thread: Green 472, 704, 907; Orange 740, 742, 971; Red 221, 900, 3328; Grey 762
15 × 20cm (6 × 8in) piece of heavyweight interfacing
25 × 33cm (10 × 13in) piece of firm white cardboard
Strong button thread
Basting thread
Rectangular wooden frame of suitable size

Carefully enlarge the design, using the grid to help you. Each square within the enlarged box must measure 27mm ($1\frac{1}{16}$in).

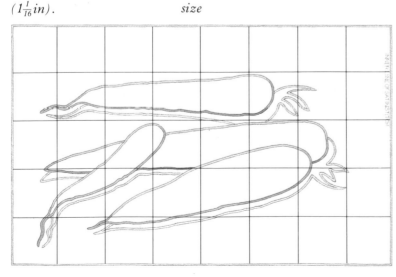

to make the carrot picture

1. Press the top fabric and backing fabric to remove any creases before stretching the two layers over the wooden frame. Make sure that the tension of the two fabrics is even and that the grain of the top, linen-type fabric lies parallel to the sides of the frame. This will ensure that the narrow green border can be worked to produce a straight rectangle that is not distorted.

2. Using the grid to help you accurately enlarge the design, make a tracing of the design and cut it out around the border edge. Place the shape in the centre of the frame, aligning the edges of the paper pattern with the grain of the fabric. Attach the pattern to the fabric with small pieces of masking tape.

With Green 472, work Satin Stitch around the edge of the paper pattern, working over five threads of fabric to give the narrow border. (See page 43 to work the corners.)

3. Baste around the shapes of the carrots and the shadows, working through the paper pattern and the fabric. Then, with the point of a pin or needle, score around the stitching to break the paper. Carefully pull away the pieces of paper, leaving the design shapes accurately stitched on the fabric.

4. Trace and cut out the four carrot shapes from the pattern, separating the shapes so that each vegetable is complete.

Pin the shapes to the interfacing and cut out.

5. Pin and baste the interfacing carrot shapes in position, overlapping them where necessary.

You can now remove the basting stitches which showed you the position of the carrots on the backing fabric, but do *not* remove the basting threads which show the shadows.

6. Measure and baste a line 3.5cm (1¼in) from the outer edge of the green border. Within this area, freely work randomly positioned carrots using Green 704 and Orange 740.

7. Now work the central area of the picture.

Make the stalks and trimmed leaves by working Stumpwork 'picots' using Green 472 and 907. Follow the instructions on page 86, where they form part of the stalks of the tomatoes. Picots are particularly suitable, as they can be twisted and arranged to look very effective.

8. Next, work the bodies of the carrots. This may seem a daunting task as they are quite large areas of solid stitchery, but if you look carefully at the illustration and keep referring to it, you will be able to gradually build up the colour and shape of each vegetable.

You will probably find it easier to begin each carrot at its tip and work upwards from here, using the three shades of orange. Use the lightest shade of Orange to show the highlighted areas.

You must work quite small Straight Stitches, positioning them so that they appear to curve around the side of the carrot shape.

Once you have worked an area using the three Orange shades 740, 742, 971, begin to add the details by using the red shades. Again, remember to study the illustration of the completed carrots to help you place your stitches. If you do not like the effect you have created, you

can always unpick some of the stitchery and rework it.

Use the very bright Red 900 sparingly as it is a very bold colour; add scattered Straight Stitches in small areas to give a speckled effect. The rusty Red 3328 is used as a shading colour around the undersides of the carrots, while the very dark Red 221 is used to emphasize the shape of the carrots while also adding the blemish marks on the vegetable skins.

Try to work with several needles in the fabric at the same time (threaded with the different colours) so that you can change from shade to shade quickly. This will also discourage you from filling in large areas in one colour.

You must look at your embroidered picture critically, as if it were a drawing or painting. Stand away from it so that you can look at it more clearly; decide if the stitchery is effective and if it is doing what you want it to do.

9. When you have completed the carrots, work the shadows in Straight Stitch along the horizontal threads of the fabric using the Grey Coton Perlé 762. Check to make sure your shadows look pleasing to the eye.

10. Remove the fabric from the frame. Place the embroidery face down on a clean, flat surface and position the

The centre still life of carrots is realistically 'painted' on the fabric with needle and thread. Each stitch helps to show the shape and form of the root vegetables.

Work three or four orange Straight Stitches which converge in a point for the carrot root and then add a few smaller green Straight Stitches for the stalks.

Previous page, the bright colours and bold shapes of the vegetables have been cheerfully translated into stitchery in these pictures.

Below right, work three short Straight Stitches for the stalks of the tiny mushrooms and then work the caps in Satin Stitch, reducing the size of the stitches to give a rounded shape.

Enlarge the mushroom design to the same size as the carrot design using the grid method.

piece of cardboard centrally over the stitched area. Trim away the surplus fabric, leaving 5cm (2in) around each side of the cardboard.

Carefully turn the cardboard and fabric over so that the embroidery is now facing you and adjust it to make sure it is still centred over the cardboard.

With dressmaking pins, secure the fabric to the cardboard, pulling and gently stretching the fabric, pushing the pins into the edge of the cardboard. You may have to remove some pins and adjust the fabric slightly to make sure the green border looks straight and regular.

Then, with a long length of button thread, lace the fabric over the cardboard, pulling the thread lightly on the wrong side.

Carefully choose a suitable frame to complement your picture of carrots.

mushroom picture

Like the carrot picture, this group of button mushrooms is set within a decorative border of randomly placed miniature mushrooms.

materials

40 × 50cm (16 × 20in) piece of white evenweave linen-type fabric such as Zweigart 'Linda' No. E1235
40 × 50cm (16 × 20in) piece of white cotton backing fabric
1 skein each DMC Coton Perlé thread No. 5: Green 472; Pink 223, 754; Beige 738, 739, 842, 951; Ecru; Grey 451, 762
Small scraps of heavyweight interfacing
25 × 33cm (10 × 13in) piece of firm white cardboard
Strong button thread
Basting thread
Rectangular wooden frame of suitable size

to make the mushroom picture

1. Follow the method for the carrot picture to step 5. Instead of working tiny carrots, work lots of mushrooms scattered around the border of Green 472, using Pink 754, and|Beige 738 and 951 (see below).

2. As with the carrot picture, you must really look closely at the stitchery of the mushrooms to see how they have been worked, and use the illustration to help you build up your own embroidery.

Have several needles threaded with the different shades so that you can change thread easily.

The direction of your stitching is very important. Within each mushroom shape there are three or four parts which need to stand out from each other. Their colouring is very similar, so it is important that the direction of the stitches makes each area distinct (see opposite).

To emphasize the frill around the base of the mushroom head, work a line of Buttonhole Stitch instead of Straight Stitch, with the bars of the stitches lying on the uneven edge to strengthen it.

Use Beige 738, 739, 842, 951, Pink 754 and Ecru to build up the mushrooms. Create the darkest areas with Grey 451 and the spotted blemishes and particles of soil with Dark Pink 223.

3. Work the shadows in Grey 762, placing the Straight Stitches along the horizontal threads of the fabric.

4. Remove the embroidery from the frame and mount it on cardboard, following step 10 of the instructions for the carrot picture.

v e g e t a b l e   g a r d e n   c u s h i o n

Vegetable gardening can provide a very attractive visual end product just as flower gardening can. Often, however, people do not consider the area of their garden that is devoted to the production of fruit and vegetables worthy of careful planning and design. It is purely custom that has led the majority of us to overlook the beauty of colour, shape and pattern that can be produced by a row of cabbages, instead of admiring it simply for the size of the vegetables and their ultimate flavour and culinary potential.

In this project, you will see that the design is based upon an intricate knot garden pattern of footpaths and hedges, giving small isolated areas for plant growth. The design is simple and bold, exploiting the rich variety of textures that can be achieved with the use of several canvaswork stitches and wool yarns of different thicknesses.

materials

50cm (20in) square of petit point canvas 7 holes per cm (17 holes per in)
130cm (52in) light grey velvet ribbon, 1cm (⅝in) wide
90cm (36in) dark grey velvet ribbon, 1cm (⅝in) wide
33cm (13in) square of small grey print cotton fabric
30cm (12in) square cushion pad
Grey sewing thread
Small scraps of heavyweight interfacing (pelmet weight)
Paterna Persian wool yarns: 6 skeins Fawn Brown 406; 4 skeins Fawn Brown 403; 2 skeins Loden Green 694; 1 skein each Loden Green 693, 692; Lime Green 670; Sunrise 811; Christmas Red 972; Cranberry 940; Cream 261
30cm (12in) square of tracing paper
40cm (16in) wooden frame
Waterproof or indelible marking pen
3.50mm (size E) crochet hook

to make the vegetable garden

1. Using the square of tracing paper, draw the quarter section of the design four times, matching the centre lines accurately to produce the complete trace-off pattern.

2. Place the paper pattern on a flat, light coloured surface (so that the design lines show up) and temporarily hold it in place with masking tape.

3. Find and mark the central vertical and horizontal threads of the canvas

Like the carrots, these button mushrooms appear to have been freshly gathered. Around them, their tiny stylized versions are worked freely to give a simple border pattern.

Quarter section of the vegetable garden: you only need to trace the geometric pattern of the footpaths and hedges, the position of the cabbages and the cauliflowers.

French Knots

Tent Stitch background

Satin Stitch worked over five threads. Reduce stitch size at corners so they look mitred

Encroaching Straight Stitch background

Blanket Stitch and French Knots for cabbages

Blanket Stitch and French Knots for cauliflowers

with the marking pen. Then using them to guide you, place the piece of canvas over the traced pattern; align the threads of the canvas with the side edges of the design. Carefully and accurately trace the positions of the velvet ribbons, the circular pattern of the hedge, the cabbages and the cauliflowers. The remaining parts of the design can be arranged by eye.

4. Mount the canvas on the wooden frame.

5. You are now ready to begin stitching.

Sew the velvet ribbons in place, using grey sewing thread and working small Stab Stitches along both edges of the ribbons. First, stitch the darker grey square shape in place, folding the ribbon carefully to produce neatly mitred corners. When you return to the first corner, trim the end of the ribbon diagonally and turn under the raw edge, stitching it securely but invisibly so that this corner looks as neat as the other three. Then stitch the light grey ribbon in position, again folding it neatly at the corners. You do not need to turn under the raw ends, simply overlap them into the circular hedge areas. The raw ends will then be covered with the French Knots of the hedge.

6. Next work the four cabbage patch areas. Using two strands of Loden Green 693, work about four or five French Knots in the centres of each cabbage, and then work Buttonhole Stitch leaves around the Knots, gradually making the leaves larger as you work outwards.

Remember that, as with all the vegetables in the garden, the cabbages should not be identical in shape and size, so try to vary them a little to give a pleasing effect.

The soil around the cabbages is worked in Fawn Brown 403, using two strands to give a rich 'lined' texture. Work Encroaching Straight Stitch diagonally across the threads of the canvas, from the corner towards the centre of the design, filling the area

completely. Your stitches do not have to be of a regular size; the aim is to cover the canvas solidly, but do not make the stitches longer than 1cm ($\frac{3}{8}$in).

7. Using French Knots and placing them close together, work the circular shapes of the hedge. Use two strands of Lime Green 670 to work a single line of Knots around the outer edge of the hedge, and then fill in the remaining area, using two strands of the sightly duller Loden Green 694. This will give you a rich bubbly texture for the hedge. Inside the four small circles produced by the hedge pattern, work four cauliflowers. These are worked in the same way as the cabbages, but use Cream 261 to build up the French Knot florets and then work the Buttonhole Stitch outer leaves in Loden Green 693 to complete the cauliflowers.

The soil areas are filled in with Encroaching Straight Stitch using Fawn Brown 403.

8. Next, work the remaining soil areas between the hedge and footpaths, using the same stitch as before, but in the lighter Fawn Brown 406, to cover the canvas completely.

Cut out twenty small beetroot shapes (see top right), using the heavyweight interfacing. Pin in place on the stitched areas. Then, using two strands of Cranberry 940, work Satin Stitch over and over each interfacing shape to give a built-up, bulbous effect. Work a few Straight Stitches to give a thin and crooked root end.

The leafy stalks are produced by using three strands of Loden Green 692 to work two Single Knot Stitches at the top of each beetroot (see page 79), trimming the strands of the wool yarn to give about 1cm ($\frac{3}{8}$in) in length.

9. Using only one strand of Fawn Brown 406, work Tent Stitch over one horizontal and one vertical thread to fill the centre circle of the design. Using the guidelines, divide the centre circle into quarters. Then fill each quarter with the stitches facing the direction

Trace around the carrot to make a pattern and template to help you cut out the interfacing shapes.

Trace around the beetroot to make a pattern and template to help you cut out the interfacing shapes.

Freely work Straight Stitch leaves to hold the chain in position. Then work French Knots for the strawberries.

indicated in the trace-off pattern.

Using the crochet hook and only one strand of Loden Green 692, work a 35cm (14in) length of single chain crochet (see below).

You will find that the single chain curls and twists, making it ideal for the twining stem of the ring of strawberry plants in the centre.

Using one strand of the same shade of green, arrange and then stitch the curling chain down onto the centre area, taking the ends of the chain down through the canvas with a large-eyed needle, to neaten and secure them. Then, with two strands of Green yarn, work small Straight Stitch leaves randomly on both sides of the chain (see page 95 below). Finally, work French Knots to represent the strawberries, using two strands of Christmas Red 972. In the centre of this section, work a few Single Knot Stitches, using three strands of Lime Green 670. Trim the strands to approximately 1.5cm (⅝in) in length.

10. Cut out eight carrot shapes (see page 95) using the heavyweight interfacing, and pin them in place on the canvas. Then using two strands of Sunrise 811, work Satin Stitch across them to give a raised effect, but not as bulbous as the beetroots. Complete them by working three Single Knot Stitches at the top of each carrot, using Lime Green 670 and trimming the loops to approximately 1.5cm (⅝in).

Using a single strand of Fawn Brown 406, work Tent Stitch around all the carrots and to a depth of five stitches around the outer grey ribbon footpaths. Work the stitches so that they lie across each corner point instead of facing in towards the centre of the design (see opposite).

Around the design, using two strands of Fawn Brown, work a band of Satin Stitch over five threads of canvas.

To make a crochet chain, start with a slip loop about 15cm (6in) from the end of the yarn.

Holding the hook in your right hand, pass it through the loop pulling the yarn to tighten it.

Controlling the yarn with your left hand, bring the hook towards you, then take it under and over the yarn in your left hand, catching it in the hook.

Holding the slip loop with the thumb and forefinger of your left hand, draw the hook with the yarn back through the slip loop to make the first chain. Repeat the last two steps until your chain is the correct length.

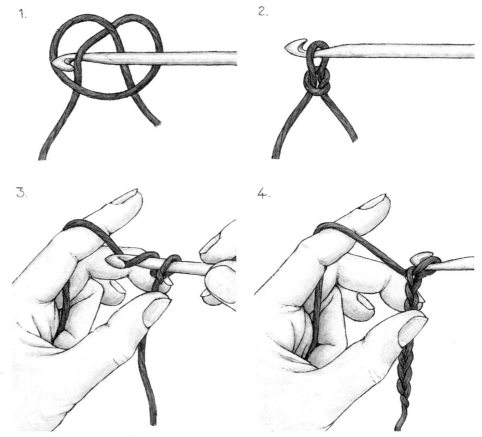

1. 2. 3. 4.

At the corners, reduce the size of the stitches to produce a mitred effect (see Satin Stitch guide on page 94).

11. Remove the canvaswork from the wooden frame and trim away the surplus canvas, leaving a 1.5cm ($\frac{5}{8}$in) seam allowance on each side of the worked area.

12. With right sides together, pin, baste and machine stitch the cushion face and back together, leave a gap at least 20cm (8in) in length on one side. Take care not to catch the tufts of the carrots when turning the corners.

Trim the excess fabric at the corners before turning to the right side. Fill with the cushion pad and neatly turn in the raw edges of the opening. Close with tiny Slip Stitches to complete the cushion. Press the back of the cushion lightly.

Velvet ribbons provide the footpaths in this delightful vegetable garden with its many varied textures, from the lumpy hearts of the cauliflowers to the fluffy fronds of the carrots.

the water garden

In a water garden the bearded iris may only very briefly burst into a display of muted colours, so why not capture them in stitchery?

Encroaching Straight Stitch builds up the colour of the leaves and petals.

*t*he inclusion of water in a garden has for hundreds of years provided delightful results and given much pleasure. A simple pond will give beautiful reflections of the colours and shapes around it, while a splashing fountain or a trickling stream will add the very special sounds that only water can provide.

When a watery environment has been successfully established, a host of plants which require such conditions can be grown and seen to flourish; around them, an entire habitat will develop which in time will support not only plants, but also a variety of wildlife.

iris towel set

To many people, the mental image of a water garden will be one of two distinct sights: graceful water-lilies floating upon the water or erect and proud clumps of irises at the water's edge.

In this project the iris has been used to decorate a hand towel and washcloth which would look delightful in any guest room. The colours used are typical of the bearded iris – soft, subtle shades which merge into the richer velvet ones.

The design is seen as a repeat pattern which could easily be used to decorate the edge of a window blind or the hem of curtains and matching tie-backs. A similar motif is also used alone on the washcloth and it too could be adapted.

materials

1 pale turquoise-green hand towel 58cm (23in) wide
1 pale turquoise-green washcloth 32cm (12½in) square
20cm (8in) matching cotton polyester, 115cm (45in) wide
20cm (8in) white cotton polyester for backing, 115cm (45in) wide
Slightly stronger turquoise-green sewing thread
Basting thread
1 skein each Anchor stranded embroidery thread: Green 267, 256, 254 (for grass); Green 260, 214, 242, 216 (for iris stems and leaves); Pink 4146, 968, 894; Rust-pink 10; Purple 99; Gold 307 (for flowers)
15cm (6in) wooden embroidery hoop

to make the borders

1. Trace the slightly smaller iris and grass motif on tracing paper, ready to transfer to the washcloth border fabric. Then trace the repeat motif on tracing paper. Also trace the parallel guidelines. Then make two photocopies facing the original way and one photocopy with the sheet of paper turned over to give a reverse or mirror image of the design.

Trim the paper away around the upper half of the iris flower so that it can be placed over the lower half of its neighbouring motif. Place the motifs together so that the mirror image copy is in between the two other copies, aligning the parallel guidelines and matching up where the design overlaps and repeats itself. Glue or tape the pieces together.

NB: If you are going to make a border strip for a larger towel, remember to make a longer repeating pattern simply by making more photocopies and joining them together.

2. Cut the turquoise-green fabric into two pieces to make a long strip measuring 70 × 20cm (28 × 8in) for the towel border and the smaller remaining piece for the washcloth. In the same way, divide the white backing fabric into two pieces with the same measurements.

3. Tape the paper patterns to a clean flat surface. Press the fabric to remove any creases. Place the turquoise-green fabric pieces centrally over the patterns and tape them to hold them temporarily.

With pale green and pink crayons, accurately trace the design on the fabric.

Remember to keep the crayons sharpened so that you can draw a fine line on the fabric without making smudgy marks.

4. Remove the fabric pieces from the paper patterns and match them to the pieces of backing fabric. With sewing thread, baste the layers of fabric together to prevent them from slipping against one another.

5. You are now ready to begin stitching.

Place your fabric in the embroidery hoop, gently pulling the fabric taut within the hoop so that the surface is smooth and flat.

6. The design is worked almost entirely in Encroaching Straight Stitch with Stem Stitch and Single Chain Stitch.

Use three strands of thread at all times.

There is no definite colour plan to follow, as a much more effective design is achieved if the flowers and foliage vary slightly from motif to motif. Basically, the grasses are worked in either of the three shades of Green 267, 256, 254. Work the stems of them in Stem Stitch. This stitch allows you to make gentle curves and yet gives a slightly thicker effect than if you use a stitch such as Back Stitch. The grass flowers are worked by grouping three small Single Chain Stitches at the tips of each short stalk end.

The stems and leaves of the irises are thick shapes tapering to a point. They need to be worked quite carefully to make sure each individual 'blade' shape is retained to stand out against its neighbour. Use the four shades of Green 260, 214, 242 and 216, working from the pointed tip in the palest shade, gradually changing to the darkest shade as you work down towards the base end. Use Encroaching Straight Stitch to fill the shapes, working the stitches to lie parallel to

the sides of the leaves and stems, staggering the length of the stitches randomly. Remember you are colouring them in as if you are using crayons.

Finally, the iris flowers are also worked in Encroaching Straight Stitch, which is ideal to build up shaded areas, as the different colours can merge together to prevent a sudden change from one shade to another which would look ugly and unnatural.

There are two colour combinations used for the flowers, so alternate them to create a pleasing effect. The middle flower of the towel border and that of the washcloth is worked using Gold 307 for the centre of the large lower petal, then Purple 99 is worked around this. Then the paler mauvish Pink 968 is worked around the purple, and finally the edge is worked in Pink 4146. The smaller petals are worked in Mauve-pink 968 and Pink 4146 shades (see illustration on page 100).

The second colour combination is worked in the same way, but the Rust-pink 10 is used instead of the deep purple, and Pink 894 replaces the mauvish Pink 968. If you wish, you can scatter a few Straight Stitches of the deepest shade around the lower petal to create a spotted effect (see washcloth detail).

Try to work the Encroaching Straight Stitches so that the stitches lie in the direction that makes the shapes look like real petals.

8. When all the stitchery is complete, press the fabric on the wrong side, using a steam iron or a water spray with a dry iron to remove any creases, as the fabric will be quite crumpled from being handled during stitching.

Then, using your paper pattern strip as a guide laid over the embroidery, draw parallel lines with a crayon on each side of the guidelines, adding 1cm (⅜in) on each side.

Using a decorative edging stitch on your sewing machine, stitch on the inner side of each drawn line along the entire length of the towel border and the washcloth border strips.

(If you do not have a decorative stitch facility on your machine, you can either turn a narrow hem, trimming the fabric on the drawn lines, or machine Satin Stitch on the inside of the lines.)

Trim away the excess fabric along the edges and also at the ends of the strips, allowing a 1cm ($\frac{3}{8}$in) turning at each end.

Press once more if necessary before pinning the strips across the end of the towel and washcloth. There may be a woven band across the towel which will detract from your embroidery. If so, place the border over it to hide it.

Pin the strips to the towelling and baste to hold, taking care to turn under the raw edges of each short end of the band to neaten and finish them.

Machine stitch around the edges to attach the borders securely.

Remove all basting threads to complete the project.

Aftercare: It will be necessary to hand-wash these items and to gently pull them into shape while damp. Press them carefully with a steam iron to encourage the embroidery to stand out and to keep the fabric flat.

Opposite, use this design for the washcloth motif.

The repeat pattern has been varied slightly to create the washcloth motif.

lily pond quilted cushion

This pastel-coloured cushion is quickly worked with great effect. The method that has been used to interpret the design is quilting, with small individually worked flowers added when the quilting is complete to give extra depth to the design.

The fabric that has been used is a furnishing fabric with a rough silky finish. In fact, it is made of a combination of viscose and acetate fibres so that it is washable and durable while being very reasonably priced.

materials

70cm (28in) piece of 152cm (60in)
   wide pale blue silk finish furnishing
   fabric
50cm (20in) square of white cotton
   backing fabric
DMC Coton Perlé thread No. 5: 1
   skein each Green 369, 943, 954, 993;
   Pale Pink 818; Pale Apricot 951

Pale green sewing thread to match 993
Pale blue sewing thread
Scraps of heavyweight interfacing (or
   white felt)
40cm (16in) square of medium-weight
   polyester batting or wadding
33cm (13in) square cushion pad
40cm (16in) square wooden frame
Fabric transfer pencil (preferably blue)
30cm (12in) square of tracing paper

to make the quilted cushion

1. If you have access to a photocopying machine, make four copies of the trace-off pattern. Trim along the dotted lines of the two 'inner' edges and very accurately join them together to make a larger square with the repeat design inside it.

Alternatively, make a tracing of the design, repeating it four times within a 30cm (12in) square.

Page 101, use this design for the border repeat pattern.

The soft, silky fabric, when quilted, produces a gently undulating effect which is used to highlight the simple repeat design of the lily pond.

2. With clear tape, secure the complete design on a flat surface and place the sheet of tracing paper squarely over it. Tape to hold it temporarily.

With a very sharp-pointed transfer pencil, carefully draw the design lines of the lily leaves and entwined stems on the tracing paper. Keep the pencil sharpened and make very fine lines on the paper, as a thicker line will become ugly and blotchy when transferred onto the fabric.

Gently brush away any specks of the pencil from the surface of the paper when you have completed the design, as they would spoil your fabric if not removed.

3. Press the blue fabric to remove any creases, and following the cutting guide, cut out two long strips across the width of the fabric each 10cm (4in) wide; one 35cm (14in) square; one 50cm (20in) square. Reserve the two strips and the smaller square to be used to assemble the cushion.

4. Following the manufacturer's instructions supplied with the pencil, carefully transfer the design onto the large square of blue fabric, centring the tracing paper face downwards over the fabric, with the edges of the paper aligned with the straight grain of the fabric.

Take great care not to move the layers while transferring the design or

it will become blurred and distorted.

5. Stretch the white backing fabric over the wooden frame, but do not pull it too taut. Then place the square of wadding (or batting) over it, trimming it to the size of the frame if necessary.

Place the top fabric over the wadding (or batting) and hold it in place by pinning it with dressmaker's pins (around the sides) to the white backing fabric.

Do not pull the blue fabric tightly, but smooth it from the centre to the sides so that you retain the puffiness while securing it in position.

6. You are now ready to begin quilting.

This particular type of quilting is called English Quilting. You have made a sandwich of the backing fabric and the blue top fabric and your layer of wadding (or batting) is the filling. When you stitch through the layers, the stitches will pinch the layers together, giving a quilted and puffy effect.

The stitch used in this project to quilt the layers together is simply a small and even Back Stitch.

Following the colour guide given on the trace-off pattern (remember you will be looking at it reversed on your fabric so if you find it easier, use a mirror to look at the colours the right way around), work from the innermost

Use this to help you cut out your fabric for the cushion.

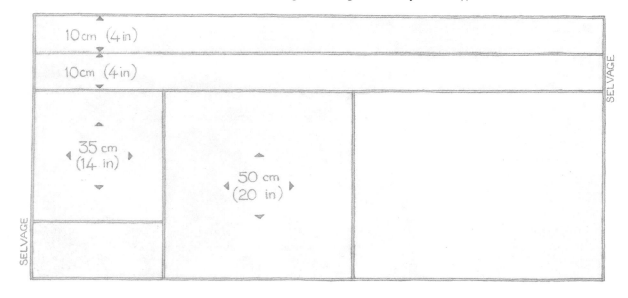

The simplified lily flowers are worked like the flowers of the Knot Garden Cushion, and are appliquéd onto the lily pond with French Knots.

areas of the design outwards. Use one hand to smooth and flatten the layers while stitching with the other hand. Remember there must be no puckers or creases in the blue fabric.

7. When you have worked all the water lily leaves and their stems, cut out forty small circles using the scraps of heavyweight interfacing. The circles should all be approximately 1.2cm ($\frac{1}{2}$in) in diameter.

Work Buttonhole Stitch around each circle so that the 'bars' of the stitches lie on the edges of the circles while the 'stems' all converge in the centres.

Work twenty circles in Pale Pink 818 and twenty in Pale Apricot 951. Reserve eight pale apricot and four pale pink flower circles. Arrange the remaining flowers on the quilting, using the trace-off pattern as a guide.

Work a Pale Green 369 French Knot in the centre of each of the flowers to attach them to the quilted fabric.

8. Using the same pale green thread, scatter tiny Straight Stitch stars randomly around the outer edges of the lily design to extend the cushion design to fill 33cm (13in) square. Also work a few stars randomly in the central area. These stars are five small Straight Stitches which all converge on one point and pull the layers of fabric and wadding together to give a soft rounded effect.

Work a single pale pink French

Knot in the centre of each star.

9. With small stitches, baste around the inner edge of the frame to pinch the layers of fabric and wadding (or batting) together before removing the quilted cushion face from the frame.

Trim away the outer edges close to the line of basting.

With your lily design centrally positioned, measure and then baste to mark a 33cm (13in) square.

10. Join the two long strips of blue fabric to make a continuous band. (Neaten the raw edges of the seams to prevent fraying.) If your sewing machine has different decorative stitches, choose one that will make a suitable edging; it must prevent fraying as well as complement the design. If your machine does not have this facility, work a machine Satin Stitch or a rolled hem.

With your chosen stitch and green sewing thread, stitch along one raw edge of the band 2cm ($\frac{3}{4}$in) away from the edge so that you can control the stitching with ease. With sharp-pointed scissors, trim away the excess fabric.

Change to pale blue sewing thread.

Along the other edge of the band, work a double line of gathering stitches, just on the outside of the 1.5cm ($\frac{5}{8}$in) seam allowance.

11. Carefully draw up the gathering threads and pin the frilled band around the cushion face with right sides facing and matching the seam lines. Arrange the frills evenly along each side and baste to hold. Machine stitch along the seam line, taking extra care at the corners.

12. With right sides together, place the cushion back over the cushion face, keeping the frill flat and facing downwards over the quilted face. Pin and baste the layers together and machine stitch along the seam line, leaving a gap of at least 15cm (6in) along one side.

Trim seam allowance and clip across the corners to remove the bulk of the excess fabric. Turn to the right side.

Opposite, either trace the quarter section of the lily pond or make photocopies of it to give the complete design.

Put the cushion pad into the quilted cover. Turn in the raw edges and hand stitch to close the gap.

13. With the remaining Green 954 Coton Perlé thread, make a long, three strand twisted cord (see Special techniques, page 135). Divide the cord into four equal lengths of approximately 45cm (18in). Remember to knot the ends before cutting the lengths to prevent the cord from unravelling. Tease out the cut ends to make small tassels.

With green sewing thread, stitch the cords along each side of the cushion on the seam lines, so that the cords hang loosely from each corner.

14. Arrange one pale pink and two pale apricot flowers at each corner and work a Pale Green 369 French Knot in the centre of each flower to attach it securely to the surface fabric at each corner of the cushion, ensuring that your stitches do not show on the reverse side of the cushion.

Join the quarter sections on the dotted lines.

Position for flowers. Do not draw on fabric.

⬭	954
⬭	369
⬭	943
⬭	993

the wild flower garden

*Appliquéd wild flower patches decorate the crisp,
white bed linen, while on the table the dainty Rose
Scented Sachet perfumes the air.*

*t*here is a steadily growing interest among gardening enthusiasts to introduce wild flowers and plants into some area of their garden. This has happened to a great extent because of a growing awareness that many such plants can grow happily within a garden. In fact, some need to be encouraged to do so, or they may become very scarce or even die out in their natural habitats, the hedgerows and meadows.

There is of course a danger that the unthinking collector of such plants might dig up and remove a wild plant from its natural habitat in order to have it in his garden. This must not happen and need not, for today a wide and varied selection of wild plant seeds is available, all of which with a little care can be nurtured into mature flowering plants.

If we think back to the earliest gardens, they were simply collections of plants brought near to the home so that they could be gathered easily for whatever medicinal or culinary purpose they were needed. So perhaps today when we introduce wild plants into our gardens, we are merely repeating what our ancestors did. Indeed, some plants such as the forget-me-not or honeysuckle, are still called 'wild', even though they have been grown as garden plants for so many years that they are also accepted as cultivated plants.

wild flower duvet cover and pillowcases

To embroider a double duvet (continental quilt) cover with matching pillowcases may at first appear to be a daunting project, taking hours of your time to complete. However, as you can see from the picture, this delightful bed linen has been decorated very effectively, but with the minimum of effort. You can appliqué as many or as few 'patches' of wild flowers as you wish and arrange them in whatever way you find pleasing. All you have to do is embroider approximately fourteen wild flower motifs and then apply them to the duvet cover and pillowcases.

Another bonus with this project is that you do not have to handle the large amounts of fabric of the cover while actually embroidering the flowers; they are worked on individual pieces of fabric in a hoop and then applied to the bed linen.

There are six different flower motifs. If you wish to add more, you can carefully trace suitable flowers from a well-illustrated wild flower book, and use this as your inspiration when matching colours and choosing stitches.

Once you have completed this beautiful project, you may be tempted to use this 'patch' idea on table linen or on the corners of your guest towels.

materials

White cotton polyester double duvet (continental quilt) cover
2 matching pillowcases
50 × 175cm (20 × 70in) piece of white cotton polyester fabric to match duvet fabric
Anchor stranded embroidery thread: 2 skeins Green 254; 1 skein each Green 214, 216, 256, 259, 267; Mauve 95, 105, 108; Blue 120, 130; Pink 60, 76, 892; Yellow 305; Red 10; Brown 903
Sewing thread to match stranded thread: Blue 130, Green 214, Mauve 108, Pink 892, 60, 76
Tissue paper
20cm (8in) wooden embroidery hoop
Pale blue, mauve, pink, green crayons

to make the cover and pillowcases

Prepare your patches by cutting the piece of fabric into fourteen 25cm (10in) squares.

Enlarge the flower squares and then trace each design on the fabric after it has been stretched in the frame.

Use three strands of embroidery thread at all times.

Work each design twice and then choose two to repeat for the pillowcases.

1 forget-me-not design

Using the trace-off pattern to guide you, work the stems, leaves and sepals using Green 214 and 267. Work the stems in small neat Stem Stitches, working three tiny Straight Stitches for the sepals where the flowers have fallen.

The leaves are worked in the same shade of green as the stem, using Fishbone Stitch (see page 48) to give a long thin shape.

Then work over the Fishbone Stitch leaf in the other shade of green in Back Stitch to represent the central vein of the leaf.

Using Blue 130, work the petals of the flowers in Straight Stitches, placing the stitches closely side by side and making them smaller at the sides of the petals (see below).

Work a large French Knot (twisting the thread four or five times around the needle) in Blue 130 to represent the flower buds at the tips of the stems. To complete the flowers, work a single French Knot in the centre of each open flower using Yellow 305.

2 dog violet design

Using the trace-off pattern and the picture as a guide, work the foliage using Green 254 and 256. The stems are worked in Stem Stitch and the small leaves on each side of the stems are then added by working a few Straight Stitches of differing lengths to give the sharp, pointed shapes.

The two green seed pods are also worked in Satin Stitch in the darker shade of Green 256 with two or three Pale Green 254 stitches to add highlights. The leaf-like shapes at the base of the two pods are then worked in the paler Green 254 in a mixture of Stem Stitch and Encroaching Straight Stitch.

The point to remember when stitching this sort of design is that the effect created is far more important than working a perfect stitch. If you have to split a stitch, coming up through it in order to place the next stitch correctly, then do so; as long as the effect is what you want, do not be afraid to experiment.

The three large leaves are worked in Pale Green 254 in Encroaching Straight Stitch, placing the stitches so that they lie pointing out towards the scalloped edge and away from the central vein. Then, when the leaf has been completely worked, add darker green Back Stitches to represent the veins.

Work the dainty flowers using Mauve 105 and 108. Work each petal shape individually in Encroaching Straight Stitch, filling the shapes by placing the stitches along the length of each petal rather than across them. Build up each petal in the paler mauve shade and then add the darker shade along the centres of the petals, so that on the open flowers the darker shaded areas all converge in the centre of each violet.

To complete the design, work two small Yellow 305 French Knots at the centre of each open flower.

Work three Straight Stitches for each flower petal of the forget-me-not and strawberry flowers.

Overleaf, the wild flowers vary in shape and form as well as colour so they require thoughtful interpretation into stitchery.

Previous page, enlarge each motif accurately, using the grid to help you. Draw the enlarged grid so that each square measures 29mm (1⅛in).

Choose your favourite motif to appliqué to the pillow case.

Work tiny Straight Stitches inside the loops of some of the Chain Stitches to add detail and interest to the clover flowers.

3 wild strawberry design

As with the previous designs, work the stems in Stem Stitch, using Green 259, 254 and 267. The small leaves are worked in a few Straight Stitches in the two lighter shades of green. The large strawberry leaves are worked in Green 254 in Satin Stitch, placing the stitches so that they lie outwards from the centre vein at an angle, and ending unevenly to give the jagged edge of the leaves. The veins are then placed on top of the closely worked Satin Stitches in the darker shade of green.

Using the illustration and trace-off pattern to guide you, work the strawberries in Red 10 and in the two lighter shades of green to show the fruits at different stages of ripening. Work lots of small French Knots clustered together to represent the slightly rough texture of the fruits.

Finally, work the petals of the strawberry flower and bud in Pink 892 in Straight Stitch in the same way as you have worked the forget-me-not flowers (see page 111). Work five Straight Stitches in Green 254 around the open flower to represent the sepals, and fill the centre of the flower with a large French Knot in Green 259, surrounded by a ring of tiny Yellow 305 French Knots.

4 bluebell design

Work the stems of the bluebells in Green 214 in a thickened Stem Stitch so that the stitches lie diagonally across the long, slender stems. (This stitch could also be described as Satin Stitch in the way it is used to fill the narrow stems diagonally.)

At the tops of the two stems where the flowers appear, continue your Stem Stitches, but reduce the size of the stitches to create the thinner stems. At the same time, work the tiny leaf shapes in Straight Stitches as you have done on the other flower designs.

Then work the large and boldly shaped leaves in Encroaching Straight Stitch, shading the leaves from the lighter shade Green 214 at the tips, through 267 and ending with Green 216 at their base. Take care to shade the leaves so that where they lie in front of one another their shapes are still well-defined. Then work the bluebells in a mixture of Blue 120 and 130, trying to use the two shades to define the bell shapes and working in a combination of Split Stitch and Satin Stitch to make the small curved areas stand out. Add two or three tiny Straight Stitches in Mauve 95 to add highlights to each flower.

5 clover design

Work the stems in Green 254 and 214 in Stem Stitch. Then work the three sharply pointed leaves in Green 254 in Fishbone Stitch. The main clover leaves are worked entirely in Satin Stitch, working each leaf in two halves and using two different shades of green (see trace-off pattern and illustration to guide you).

The clover flowers are worked in Single Chain Stitches grouped closely together and arranged in rows. Work from the flower tip towards the stalk, using Pale Pink 892 and then gradually change to the deeper Pink 60.

To break up the colours and add a little more interest, add a few tiny Straight Stitches to fit into the loops of the Chain Stitches using the contrast-

ing shade of Pink 74 (see below left). Then work three small Single Chain Stitches at the base of the flower, in the same shade of green as that used for the flower stem.

6 heather design

This is probably the quickest and most freely worked of all the designs. Work the stems in Brown 903, working thin curved lines of Stem Stitch. Then, using the two dark Green shades 216 and 267, work lots of tiny Straight Stitches radiating out from the stems, converging in clusters at intervals along the stems. The positions of these clusters are given on the trace-off pattern, but not the individual leaves, which can be freely worked by eye.

At the lower ends of the stems, you will find that the spiky leaves will overlap and become quite dense. Try to keep some order among them. When you feel satisfied with the effect achieved with the green Straight Stitches, work the tiny bell-like flowers of the heather in Satin Stitch, using predominantly Pink 60, with a few Mauve 95 flowers scattered among the others. To create the frilled lower edge of the flowers, work four small Straight Stitches in the same colour as the main part of the flower, pointing outwards at different angles. Finally, add one minute Brown Straight Stitch below the frilled edge to complete the design.

to appliqué the patches

When you have worked all your patches, press them on the wrong side to remove any creases and make the stitchery more pronounced on the right side. Trim away the excess fabric along the marked cutting lines to give the exact size of the finished patch.

Place the duvet cover over the double bed and arrange the patches in a pleasing way on top of the bed. Lightly pin the patches in position before carefully lifting the cover from the bed and placing it on a large, clean, flat surface.

Use a decorative machine stitch to appliqué the patches to the bed linen.

Pin and baste the patches to the upper surface of the duvet cover by placing a piece of cardboard in between the layers, moving it around so that it is under each of the patches as you attach them.

Using a decorative edging stitch or a wide Satin Stitch, machine along the edges of the patches, ensuring that the raw edge is covered and secured by the stitching.

Use the blue sewing thread for the forget-me-not patches; the mauve thread for the dog violet patches; the very pale pink thread for the wild strawberry patches; the green for the bluebell patches; the mid-pink thread for the clover patches and the bright pink thread for the heather patches.

Arrange the last two patches in the top right hand corners of the two pillowcases. Do not place them too near the corners, as it will then be difficult to stitch them on the sewing machine.

When stitching around the patches, place a piece of tissue paper under the area to be stitched. It prevents the fabric from stretching and puckering and is particularly useful when appliquing one piece of fabric to another when their grain does not match. The tissue will fall away under the patch once it has been stitched.

Securely fasten off all the threads on the wrong side of the cover and the pillowcase to complete this eye-catching project.

wild flower cushion

Blue and yellow always complement each other, and in this beautiful cushion the two have been used with great effect to emphasize these very small wild flowers that could so easily appear insignificant.

The flowers are the tiny blue forget-me-not, often associated with true love and faithfulness, and the bright yellow, early flowering lesser celandine which carpets woodland all over the British Isles.

Both flowers lend themselves to being represented in stitchery within the three areas of this delightful design.

The centre area of the cushion is a small block of Cathedral Window patchwork which gives isolated areas of fabric ideal for tiny embroidered motifs to be worked within them. Around this is a muted yellow print fabric which has been linked to the design theme by colour and by the addition of randomly worked forget-me-not flowers. Then around the outside edge is a border design, repeated on each side and composed of trailing stems of the two plants.

Velvet ribbons have been used to bring strength of colour and a certain richness to the design and also to hide all the raw edges of the fabrics.

As with many other projects, the stitches used are few and simple.

materials

50cm (20in) piece of pale blue cotton fabric, 90cm (36in) wide
12.5cm × 40cm (5 × 16in) piece of very pale yellow cotton fabric
50cm (20in) square of white cotton backing fabric
38cm (15in) piece of wide muted yellow print cotton fabric, 150cm (60in) wide
105cm (41in) golden yellow velvet ribbon, 1cm (⅜in) wide
70cm (28in) forget-me-not blue velvet ribbon, 1cm (⅜in) wide
160cm (63in) forget-me-not blue velvet ribbon, 1.5cm (⅝in) wide
160cm (63in) narrow piping cord suitable for wider ribbon
5 × 1cm (⅜in) diameter self-cover buttons
Golden yellow, pale blue and forget-me-not blue sewing thread
DMC stranded embroidery thread:
2 skeins each Blue 827, 809; Green 320, 3347; 1 skein each Yellow 742, 725
36cm (14in) square cushion pad
50cm (20in) square sheet of dressmaker's graph paper
Fabric transfer pencil (preferably blue)
Suitable square wooden frame

to make the cushion

1. Begin with the Cathedral Window patchwork section.

The name given to this type of patchwork refers to the circular patterns that are created by using two different fabrics, which echo the beautiful patterns often seen in stained glass windows. It is also called Mayflower patchwork.

The key to success with this type of patchwork, as with any other, is accuracy in cutting out, in folding and preparing and in stitching the fabrics. If the pieces are not all prepared and assembled with great care, the end product will be distorted and unappealing.

Cut a 50cm (20in) square from the pale blue fabric and set it aside to make the main body of the cushion.

From the remaining fabric, accurately cut out four 15cm (6in) squares, making sure that you cut them so that their edges are parallel to the grain of the fabric. Similarly, cut out twelve 4.5cm (1¾in) squares using the pale yellow fabric. (Use the squared graph paper to make two templates to ensure the shape and size is accurate.)

Trim the larger paper template to measure 14cm (5½in) square. Place this on top of one of the blue fabric squares so that you have an equal amount of fabric showing around the paper. Fold this over the paper edge, taking care

Narrow velvet ribbons are used to hide the raw edges of fabric shapes as well as to emphasize the designs, while the tiny embroidered buttons are a charming surprise.

not to fold the paper as well, and press it to give a neat square, remove the paper leaving the edges turned.

Fold the fabric square in half lengthways and widthways, finger-pressing it to show where the centre is. Then open it out and fold the four points into the centre, hiding the narrow, turned edge (see step 1).

With pale blue sewing thread, make a few tiny stitches to hold the points in place at the centre and once more press it carefully (step 2). Repeat this process once more, folding the corners into the centre and stitching them (step 3).

Repeat this with the other three blue fabric squares. Then with the folded sides together and using Whip Stitch, sew the four pieces together to form a larger square (step 4). Press flat (step 5).

Place the small yellow squares over the slightly larger blue squares that have been formed by folding and stitching the pieces together (step 6). You will find that as you turn back the folded blue edges over the raw edges of the yellow squares, the blue edge will

curve gently into an arc. Stitch this curved edge with matching thread through all layers to hold the yellow square in place. The inner four pieces can be stitched on all sides, but the outer eight ones can only be stitched on two sides.

2. Press the white and blue squares of fabric to remove any creases. Laying the blue piece over the white, baste them together.

On the sheet of squared graph paper, draw a 36cm (14in) square to represent the seam line of the cushion. In the middle of this, draw a 25cm (10in) square. Cut around these lines so that you have a paper pattern of the border (see below). Pin this to the layers of

Draw the outer square 36cm (14in) and the inner square 25cm (10in) on squared graph paper.

The fabric must be very carefully prepared for the Cathedral Window patchwork. Working methodically through the steps, make sure every fold is accurate.

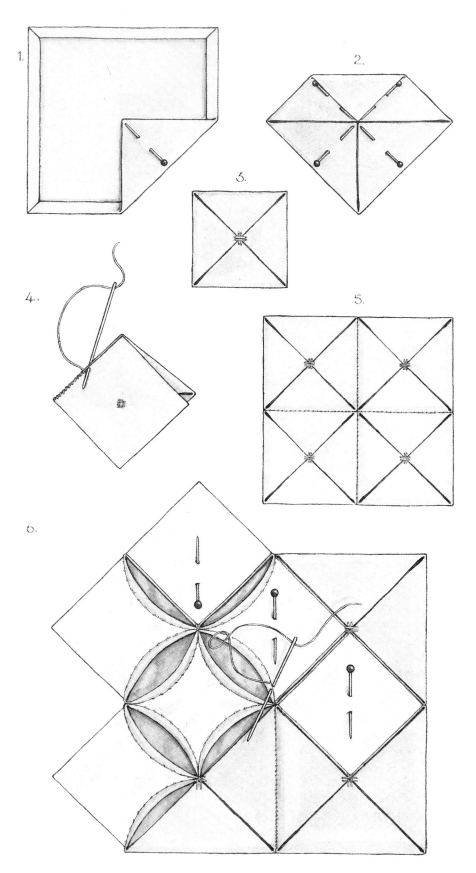

Pin the small yellow squares over the slightly larger blue squares that have been formed. Turn back the folded blue edges and stitch in place.

fabric (matching the grain of the fabric with the pattern sides).

Baste around the paper pattern, keeping your stitches close to the paper edge. Remove the pattern.

3. From the muted yellow fabric, cut twice across its width, from selvage to selvage, to give two long strips, each 10cm (4in) wide. Reserve these for the frilly edge of the cushion.

From the remaining fabric, cut a 38cm (15in) square and set it aside to make the back of the cushion.

Then cut a 25cm (10in) square. Place it on top of the blue fabric so that it fits exactly within the smaller basted square. Pin and baste to hold, keeping all fabric layers smooth and flat against one another.

Pin and baste the golden yellow ribbon around the edge of the yellow fabric so that the outer edge just covers the raw edge of the yellow fabric. Leave 1cm ($\frac{3}{8}$in) extra at the first corner. When you reach the next corner, fold the ribbon carefully to produce a sharp right-angle turn and a 'mitred' look to it. Repeat with the next two corners. The ribbon at the last corner needs to be carefully trimmed (both at the beginning and end of it) so that it appears to be the same as the other three. To do this, trim the beginning of it straight across at the corner, but cut the end of it at an angle, allowing a small turning which you tuck under to hide the raw edge.

Hand stitch this securely to hold it in place. Then with matching sewing thread, machine stitch around both sides of the ribbon, keeping as close to the edge as possible.

Place the central patchwork in the middle of the square (see page 117) with the outer yellow patches laid flat. Pin the narrow blue velvet ribbon around the square shape of the patchwork piece, turning the corners neatly as you have done with the yellow ribbon. Then baste the inner edge only and machine stitch it in matching sewing thread. Lift up the ribbon and carefully trim away the excess fabric of

809
827
320
3347
742
725

Trace-off pattern for half of the flower border. Accurately trace this and then turn the paper over, matching up the stems at the centre. Then trace the design once more to give the second half of the border motif.

the yellow patches before stitching around the outer edge. Neaten and finish the fourth corner as before.

4. Stretch the cushion face over the wooden frame. If you have prepared and joined all the pieces carefully, you will find that it will not be distorted.

5. Make a tracing of the border design (see above).

Do not draw the petals of the flowers; mark only their centres. Then using the fabric transfer pencil (with a very fine

point), carefully redraw it on another piece of tracing paper.

It is always advisable to make a test piece when using a transfer pencil, so that you know whether you are using it too heavily (which makes strong, blotchy marks) or too lightly (which makes very faint marks). Following the manufacturer's instructions, transfer the design to one side of the border, positioning it centrally.

Repeat this on the other three sides.

Using three strands of embroidery thread throughout, work each border design in the same way.

All the stems are worked in small, neat curving lines of Stem Stitch. Use Green 320 for the stems of the forget-me-nots, adding a few tiny Straight Stitches at intervals along the stems. Use Green 3347 for the stems and leaves of the lesser celandine flowers. The leaves are worked in Fishbone Stitch (see page 48), which lends itself ideally to the shape required.

Work the forget-me-not flowers in Blue 809, working five small detached Chain Stitches around each flower centre. The buds at the ends of the stems are simply blue French Knots. The centres of the flowers are also single French Knots worked in Yellow 742. Similarly, the centres of the lesser celandine flowers are clusters of French Knots worked in Yellow 742, and around each cluster are tiny Detached Chain Stitch petals worked in Yellow 625.

6. Using Blue 827 and Yellow 742, scatter single forget-me-not flowers over the yellow print to link it with the rest of the design.

7. Carefully embroider a tiny forget-me-not flower on five scraps of pale yellow fabric using the same colours. Following the manufacturer's instructions cover the self-cover buttons. Sew one at each corner of the blue velvet border and one in the centre of the Cathedral Window patchwork.

8. Work the sprigs of forget-me-not and lesser celandine in the four centre patches (see right), and around the

CENTRE

CENTRE

Opposite, like a kaleidoscope pattern, this beautiful design moves from simple floral borders via a random pattern into the intricate centre panel of Cathedral Window patchwork with its minutely detailed flower motifs.

Work tiny sprigs of flowers like these within the four yellow sections of the patchwork.

edges work a single celandine flower in the four half patches next to the forget-me-not sprigs and three forget-me-not flowers in each of the remaining half patches (see page 117).

9. Remove the cushion face from the wooden frame.

10. To make the velvet edging, fold the wide blue ribbon in half over the thin piping cord. Hold the cord tightly inside the ribbon, and baste along the length of it as close to the cord as possible.

Leaving a little extra ribbon at the first corner, baste the piped ribbon along the basted seam line, carefully easing it around the corner, making it as sharp as possible. When you return to the first corner, baste both the beginning and the end of the ribbon

Baste and machine stitch the ends of the piped ribbon across each other to neaten them.

down across each other (see above). Machine stitch around the cushion face on the seam line to attach the velvet edging.

11. Make the frill to go around the cushion by joining the two long strips of yellow print fabric with two narrow seams to form a continuous band. Around one edge, work a forget-me-not blue decorative edging, using a suitable machine stitch (trim away the excess fabric), or turn under a very narrow hem and top stitch it neatly.

Around the other edge, work two lines of gathering stitches. Draw up the lines of gathering, then pin and baste the frill on the seam line around the cushion face, carefully turning the corners. Machine stitch around the seam line.

Finally, place the remaining square of yellow print fabric over the cushion face, with right sides together, carefully tucking in the frill away from the line of stitching. Machine stitch on the seam line using the previous lines of stitching to ensure accuracy. Leave an opening along one side of at least 20cm (8in).

NB: You will find it easier to use a zipper foot attachment on your sewing machine when attaching the velvet edging, frill and backing because of the ridge caused by the piping cord within the ribbon is too bulky to pass under the ordinary machine foot.

Carefully turn the cushion cover to the right side and gently ease it into shape. Place the cushion pad inside it and then Slip Stitch the edges of the opening together to complete this beautiful cushion.

h o n e y s u c k l e   t a b l e   l i n e n

The simple sprig of honeysuckle will not take long to work in one corner of the napkin.

This beautiful table linen need not take you a great deal of time as you can choose how much you wish to embroider. For example, if you want to use the cloth to cover a small table in the corner of a room you need only decorate one corner of the cloth. However, if you want to use the cloth for a larger table, repeat the motif in each corner and use the smaller design to decorate the matching napkins.

The tiny ladybirds on the twisted stems of the honeysuckle add charm and interest to the design.

m a t e r i a l s

*Pale green square or rectangular
tablecloth of the desired size
Matching napkins
To work one large and one small motif:*

Tiny ladybirds walk along the curved stems of the wild honeysuckle and stamens fall from the blooms to complete this enchanting corner motif.

DMC stranded embroidery thread: 1 skein each Green 367, 989, 3347, 3348; Pink 224, 761, 950; Yellow 745, 972; Red 351; Dark Grey 844
Pink and green crayons
Large sheet of tracing paper
20cm (8in) wooden embroidery hoop

to make the table linen

1. Carefully trace the design on tracing paper, adding the dotted guidelines. Then place the paper over a hard white surface and tape it in position.

Place one corner of the tablecloth over the design so that the pale green dotted guidelines are parallel to the edges of the cloth, but are approximately 5cm (2in) away from the fabric edge. Tape the cloth temporarily in position, and with green and pink crayons, accurately trace the design on the fabric.

If you find you cannot see the design through the green fabric, use a fabric transfer pencil to draw the design on the other side of the tracing paper and transfer it to the fabric, following the manufacturer's instructions.

Similarly, trace the napkin motif in one corner of the napkin, placing it with the stem tips pointing into the point of the corner.

2. Position the area to be embroidered in the hoop.

Use three strands of embroidery thread at all times unless otherwise indicated.

Follow the colour key of the trace-off pattern, and work the leaves and stems of the honeysuckle in a combination of the two groups of green shades. The stems are all worked in neatly curving lines of small Stem Stitches. The leaves are worked in Satin Stitch, placing the stitches so that they lie pointing down

from the tip of each leaf towards the stem and the centre of each leaf. The mature leaves are worked in two halves, working one half in one green and the other half in the other shade. The tiny buds which appear along the stems are worked in one of the two shades in small French Knots.

3. The ladybirds are worked in Satin Stitch using Red 351. To give a slightly raised effect, work a line of tiny Back Stitches around the shape of the insect's body before working Satin Stitches across it. Then work a few Satin Stitches in Dark Grey 844 to make the head of the ladybird and tiny Straight Stitches over the red of the body to give the seven spots. It is important that you keep your stitches small and neat when working the ladybirds; if you are not pleased with the effect created, remember you can quickly and easily remove the stitches and rework them.

4. The small clusters of flowers which are not yet open are all worked in the three shades of Pink 224, 761 and 950, working a line of Back Stitch around the shapes and working Satin Stitches across each shape, placing the stitches closely and evenly together and slanting them slightly from tip to base of each shape.

Work a few French Knots using Green 3348 in the centre of each flower cluster.

5. The two flower clusters in the larger motif which have fully open flowers are worked with the same shades of pink used earlier for the immature flowers.

Work the open flowers in Encroaching Straight Stitch, using a combination of the shades of pink together with Yellow 745 to give a shaded effect, with the pink in the centre of the flower turning into yellow around the edges. Work the stitches over one another and split them if necessary along the length

Trace-off pattern for the tablecloth motif.

⬭	3348
⬭	3347
⬭	989
⬭	367
⬭	351
⬭	950
⬭	224
⬭	761
⬭	745
⬭	972
⬭	844

The muted colours of the delicately embroidered corner motifs of wild honeysuckle table linen complement the light-hearted tea cosy which shows a tiny house with its window boxes crammed full of flowers.

of the shapes to give a realistic effect. Remember you are drawing or painting with your threads.

Work a few French Knots in the centre of the flower clusters using Green 3348.

6. Finally, work the stamens and pistils of the open flowers, using two strands of Yellow 972. Work the 'stalks' in tiny Stem Stitches, finishing the stamens

with a French Knot and similarly finish the pistils as indicated with a Green 3348 French Knot.

Work the small napkin motif in the same way.

7. Remove the fabric from the hoop and carefully press it on the wrong side with a steam iron to remove any creases and to give an embossed effect to the stitchery.

Trace this motif for the napkin.

special techniques and tips

One of the joys of embroidery is that there is not a great deal of equipment needed to produce a beautiful piece of work. Also, it is possible to begin embroidery with a limited number of items, and then as your interest grows, you can gradually add to your equipment and stocks of fabric and yarn.

For example, you may begin with only one or two embroidery hoops and then collect more of different sizes, as well as rectangular frames.

Always take care of the equipment that you use for your embroidery, especially scissors, which become blunt very quickly if they are used to cut paper. It is always tempting to cut paper with sharp trimming scissors if they are close to hand, but do not give in, as paper-cutting really does spoil them for cutting fabric.

It is important to keep everything very clean and damp-free; a dusty embroidery hoop will leave a mark on any fabric that is placed in it, possibly spoiling many hours of work. Similarly, a rusty needle or pin will mark, damage or ruin a piece of work. So store everything very carefully and discard anything that may spoil your work.

Your sewing basket should include a good selection of basic sewing items, such as a variety of crewel and tapestry needles as well as ordinary sewing needles, fine crochet hooks, scissors labelled to remind you of their uses, thimbles, marking pencils of different colours, etc., plus all your own personally gathered favourites that you find so useful.

fabrics

Try to collect a good selection of fabrics. You will notice that many of the projects in this book call for relatively simple, inexpensive fabrics such as cotton or cotton polyester; those fabrics which are more costly are used economically so that none of the projects is too expensive, and you will find that all can be used in a variety of ways.

Always back your fabric where it is recommended in the instructions, as the extra layer (usually of a similar weight to the top fabric) will give more body to the top layer, strengthening it and making handling easier.

However, remember that you must baste the two layers together carefully with diagonal basting stitches (see page 134) if the embroidery is to be worked freely in the hand or in a hoop. If it is to be worked on a frame, you need not baste the layers together (unless instructed to do so) as the fabrics are mounted layer by layer on the frame.

If the fabric you are using is very soft and flimsy, you can use spray starch on the wrong side to stiffen it slightly, ready for working. Spray starch can also be used on the finished stitchery if you want a very crisp, fresh, well-laundered look, such as on the Tulip Tray Cloth (see page 63).

Always test spray starch on a spare piece of fabric to ensure it is suitable, as it may leave spots on some fabrics.

threads and yarns

With the growing popularity of needle-crafts and embroidery, there is a similar growth in the availability of all the various threads and yarns that are recommended.

Most of the threads are made of cotton or wool, and the range of colours is extensive.

Always consider the type of thread in relation to the effect you wish to achieve. Some threads can be divided, giving a very fine and delicate effect or a thicker one; others cannot be split, as their fibres are twisted together when they are being spun. Also there is a difference between matt, hairy woollen yarns and the lustrous, shiny effect of cotton yarns. If you are in doubt about the effect you wish to achieve, make a few test stitches on a spare piece of fabric.

The following threads are used in this book:

Stranded thread (sometimes known as embroidery floss) is a slightly lustrous thread of six loosely twisted strands which can be separated and used singly or in any combination.

Coton Perlé or pearl cotton is a twisted thread with a rich, shiny appearance. It cannot be divided, but is available in three slightly different thicknesses: no. 8, the finest; no. 5, slightly thicker and most commonly available; and no. 3, the thickest.

Soft embroidery cotton is the thickest of the cotton threads, similar to some types of crochet cotton, with a dull, matt finish. It is a very soft thread and cannot be divided.

Tapisserie or tapestry wool is a non-divisible four-ply woollen yarn which is ideal for canvaswork and is available in a vast range of colours.

Persian yarn is a three-stranded yarn of two-ply wool that can be used singly or in combination, allowing you flexibility of thickness while you work with the same colour. Also attractive speckled effects can be achieved by mixing strands of slightly different shades.

There are, of course, many other less common embroidery threads you could use.

embroidery frames

Using a frame will be very helpful to you, and your embroidery will be more successful and have a professional look when finished if you do. It is not only easier to handle fabric that is held taut within a frame, but you will find your stitches are well-formed. If it is necessary for stitches to be of an even size or spacing, this can be done much more easily by using a hoop. Also distortion of the fabric caused by pulling yarn or thread too tightly through the fabric is reduced to a minimum.

There are a variety of frames available, and the choice depends upon the type of fabric, size of project and personal preference.

In most projects the type and size of frame you need is given to assist you.

The following frames have been used:

Rectangular frames:
    40cm (16in) square
    23cm (9in) square
    36 × 50cm (14 × 20in)
Rotating or tapestry frame:
    30cm (12in) square
Embroidery hoops:
    12.5cm (5in) diameter
    15cm (6in) diameter
    20cm (8in) diameter
    25cm (10in) diameter
    Of all of them, the 40cm (16in) square frame and the 20cm (8in) round hoop are the most useful.

Embroidery hoops Hoops are used for small pieces of embroidery worked on plainweave fabrics that will not become permanently distorted when pulled taut within the round frame. (Fabrics such as nonwoven felt or needlepoint canvas are unsuitable.)

129

*A circular embroidery
hoop is ideal for small
pieces of stitchery, repeat
patterns and borders.*

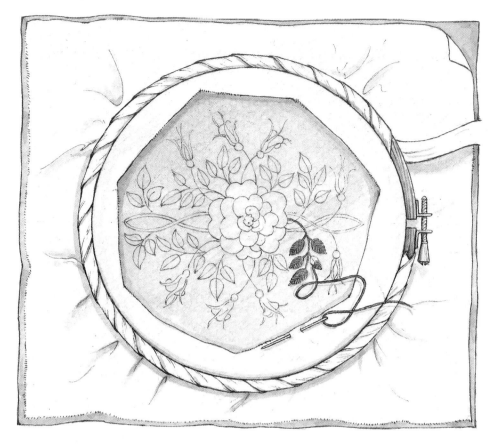

Wooden hoops are preferable to the less rigid plastic ones, and many different sizes are available. It is advisable to collect several sizes, as they are inexpensive and you can then simply select the most suitable one to use for each project.

Fabric tape wound around the outer ring of the hoop will protect soft fabrics and stitchery from the hard wooden edge. The extra layer of tape will also ensure that you get a taut working area, as it prevents the fabric from sagging while it is being worked.

Similarly, an extra layer of spare fabric placed on top of the working fabric, mounted in the hoop and then carefully cut away to reveal the area of stitchery, will protect the stitched fabric from the risk of being soiled during handling (see above).

Rectangular frames Frames are very useful for larger pieces of embroidery and canvas needlepoint. They can be made quickly and simply from lengths of whitewood 2×2cm ($\frac{3}{4} \times \frac{3}{4}$in). The corners can be butted or mitred and held firmly together with wood adhesive glue and nails.

Old, clean picture frames of soft wood can also be useful and inexpensive. Alternatively, use readymade artists' stretchers.

The fabric is stretched and fastened on this type of frame with staples or drawing pins (thumb tacks). Start at the centre of opposite sides and work towards the corners, carefully pulling and fixing the fabric so that it is evenly taut and secure on the frame.

Specialist frames (slate or rotating frames) These frames are more expensive, but they can be of great use as they are adjustable and you can stretch fabric very evenly on them. The Town Garden Tie-back (see page 71) is worked on a rotating frame, as the long, thin strip of canvas can be rolled around the rotating sides of the frame and repositioned as necessary.

enlarging a design

You will find that some of the designs in this book need to be enlarged to the correct size for working. This can be done successfully by the following 'grid' method, but accurate measuring is important.

Place the small design within a box and draw a grid of squares over it (this may already be done for you). Draw a larger box with the same proportions, but of the required size. Draw the same number of bigger squares within this (see page 132).

Copy the small design, square by square, onto the larger grid, marking where design lines cross grid lines. Join up all these marks (see page 132).

A quick way of enlarging a design can be achieved by using a photocopy machine, many of which now have the capacity to change the size of documents and drawings.

transferring designs

Once you have drawn your design to the correct size or repeated it for a border pattern, you will need to transfer it from the tracing paper to the fabric. There are several ways of doing this, and it is important to choose the most suitable method for each project. For example, if you have a very fine fabric such as cotton lawn, there is no need to baste the design onto the fabric through tracing paper, as you will be able to draw it straight onto the semi-transparent fabric.

Always use the method of transfer that is suggested to you in the projects, unless of course you have chosen to adapt the project in some way.

The following methods of transfer have been used:

direct tracing onto fabric

This is a quick and accurate method, but the fabric must be thin enough for you to see the drawn design underneath it.

Always use masking tape to secure the drawn design on a clean white surface. (If you place it on a dark surface, you will not see the design lines easily.) Then tape the fabric in position over the design so that it is smooth and flat. Then, using crayons or pencils of appropriate colours, trace the design lines carefully on the fabric. Remember to keep the crayons well-sharpened and make the finest lines possible on your fabric.

Never use lead pencil, ballpoint, felt-tipped or ink pens, as they all will leave blotchy marks on your fabric and will run if washed. The light use of crayons will not spoil the fabric, and they will wash out easily if the embroidery is laundered.

If you find it hard to see the design through the fabric, but wish to use this method, try taping the drawn design and then the fabric to a window. Remember, though, do not press too hard on the glass.

Some of the canvaswork projects are worked by drawing the design directly onto the canvas by the same method. However, you should use a waterproof or indelible marking pen to draw on the canvas, as you need a more definite mark than a crayon can give, and you will stitch over the marks. Always try to align straight lines in the design with the threads of the canvas, unless they lie at an obvious angle to them.

using fabric transfer pencils

These are useful if the fabric you are going to use is too thick or dark to see through. However, they must be used very carefully, as their colours are quite strong, and it is sometimes difficult to use them for very small detailed shapes. Always choose a pencil near in colour to either your fabric or

Draw a grid of squares over the small design, then draw a diagonal line through the grid, extending it to make a larger box of the same proportions as the small one, but enlarged to the required size.

Then draw a grid of the same number of squares in the big box. Copy where the design lines intersect the grid lines and then carefully and accurately join them up to give the enlarged design.

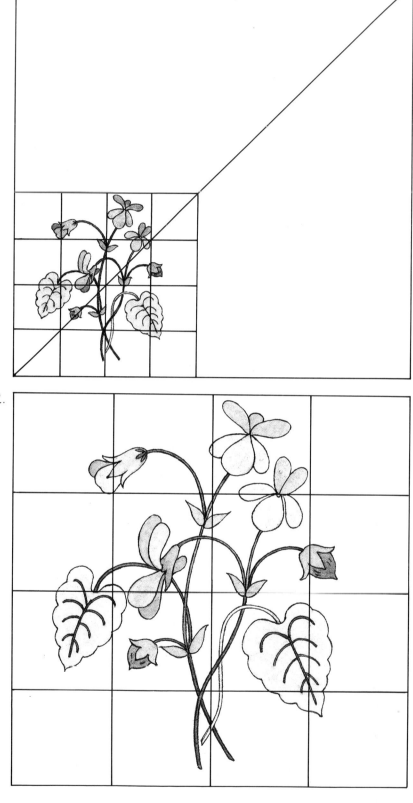

threads to reduce the risk of showing under the stitchery. Always work with a sharp-pointed pencil.

The method is simple to carry out, but always make a test sample first to ensure it will be suitable for your particular fabric.

Draw the design in pencil or felt-tipped pen on tracing paper. Then on the underside, draw along the lines once more, this time with the fabric transfer pencil. Check there are no specks of pencil left on the paper before placing it transfer side down over your fabric. Then, without moving the paper at all, carefully iron over the design area, so that the heat of the iron transfers the design onto the fabric.

using fabric dye crayons

There are several types of fabric dye crayons available from good craft shops, usually sold in small packets of at least eight different colours.

They provide a quick, clean and dry method of printing colourful designs onto fabric. Some of these crayons should be used on natural fabrics only, while others are recommended for use with synthetic or cotton mix fibres.

The type that are preferable for use in some of the projects in this book are known as Fabric Transfer Crayons. They are used like transfer pencils to draw on tracing paper; very detailed effects can be achieved.

Draw the design on tracing paper using the crayons, mixing their colours as necessary. Then place the coloured design, waxy side down, over the fabric, and without moving the two layers, iron over the coloured area to transfer it to the fabric.

Points to remember when using these crayons:
1. Draw the design in pencil on one side of the tracing paper; then colour in the other side of the paper.
2. Use a synthetic or mixture fabric as Fabric Transfer Crayons do not work well on natural fabrics.
3. Always make a test strip of colour shade and strength.
4. Keep the crayons clean and with well-shaped points.
5. Do not allow smudging to occur when drawing with the crayons on the paper as this will show on the fabric.
6. Lightly brush off any specks of crayon left on the paper (any specks left on the paper will be transferred to the fabric and possibly spoil your work).
7. Pin and hold the tracing paper firmly in position over the fabric. Do not allow the two to move against one another or a blurred effect will occur.
8. Always read and follow the manufacturer's instructions very carefully, as some types may differ from others.

tracing and basting

This method takes a little time, but sometimes it is necessary. For example, you may want to mark the shape or position of a design without marking the fabric with a pen or crayon.

Draw the design on tracing paper using a fine felt-tipped pen. Do not use lead pencil or a ballpoint pen, as the colour may pass through onto the fabric when it is stitched and leave a permanent mark.

Lay the traced design over your fabric and pin it to hold. With basting thread, work small basting stitches through the paper and fabric along all the design lines. Remember your stitches will need to be quite small in order to show the design clearly on the fabric.

When you have completed the stitching, carefully score along the stitched lines with the point of your needle to break the paper. Then gently pull away all the pieces of paper, leaving the basting stitches on the fabric as a guide. Do not distort the basting stitches as you pull. Remember to remove the basting stitches if they show when your embroidery is completed.

using a template

These are simple shapes usually made of thin cardboard or firm paper. They are made by tracing the pattern shape and transferring it to the cardboard. The shape is cut out and then used as a rigid pattern to draw around on fabric.

This method is particularly useful when the same shape is to be repeated several times in a design.

working from a chart

With some canvaswork or evenweave embroidery, the most effective way of transferring the design from paper to fabric is by carefully following the design pattern, stitch by stitch, from a colour or symbol chart. You must work systematically when following a chart, and it is vital to keep checking that you are reading the chart correctly.

Sometimes you will find it best to start in the centre of the design and sometimes at the corner of, for example, a border. However, it is always advisable to find and mark the centre of both the chart and your canvas or fabric before beginning any work.

using a g-cramp

Using a G-cramp: with your frame protruding over the edge of a table and held firmly in place by the G-cramp, you will have both hands free for sewing.

A carpenter's G-cramp, also known as a C-clamp, can greatly assist you if your embroidery is stretched on a rectangular frame. Without the cramp you have to hold the frame firmly in one hand, leaving only one hand free to stitch with. However, if you fix the frame securely to the edge of a table with the cramp, you will find that both hands are free so that you can stitch much more quickly and feel more comfortable.

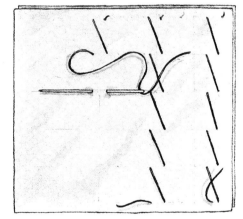

diagonal basting stitch

Diagonal Basting stitch worked in several lines across two or more layers of fabric will stop them from moving against each other.

Basting is a technique that many people try to ignore. They use pins to hold layers of fabric together, thinking it will save time and serve the purpose of basting adequately. This may work sometimes, but when you are embroidering through two layers of fabric held in the hand, it is necessary to ensure the layers are held together and will not slip away from one another, causing puckering and possibly spoiling the work. This is a particular risk if you know you will have to reposition the embroidery hoop.

Diagonal Basting is quick to work yet very worthwhile.

1. Smooth the layers of fabric together on a clean, flat surface, matching edges and wherever possible, the grains to prevent uneven stretching.

2. With a long length of basting thread, work lines of stitches (see above). Try not to lift up the fabric layers from the

working surface, but stab the needle into the layers, lifting the fabric only a little, making a small stitch under the fabric and then moving downwards over the fabric to make a long 2.5cm (1in) slanting stitch.

3. Make several lines of basting stitches across the expanse of fabric at regular intervals approximately 7.5cm (3in) apart.

making a twisted cord

Twisted cords in the same colour as one of the yarns used in a piece of embroidery will greatly enhance the work, as it will obviously match the colour scheme and yet is quick and easy to make.

Cut three or more lengths of the chosen yarn, 2½ to 3 times the finished length of the cord required. Knot the lengths together at one end and loop them around a closed door handle (or get a friend to hold them tightly). Knot the other ends together securely and pass a pencil through the loop that has been made. Wind the pencil round and

round so that the yarn twists. Continue doing this, keeping the yarn taut until it coils around itself when it is slackened slightly. Then carefully bring the two knotted ends together so that the two halves of the yarn twist tightly around one another. Gently pull and ease the cord until it is evenly twisted. Knot the ends together to prevent them from unravelling.

A thin cord, suitable for edging a cushion or tie-back, can be made by using three lengths of Coton Perlé No. 5. For a thicker cord, use more lengths of thread, or select a thicker yarn.

making a tassel

Take a length of thread or yarn 91cm (36in) long. Fold this in half four times to give a bundle of threads (see step 1 below).

Take a second length of thread, double it and pass it through a large-eyed needle (see step 2 below).

Hold the double thread around the bundle of threads and pass the needle through the loop (see step 3 below).

Pull it up tightly, then pass the needle down through the bundle and

cut it off at the end of the other threads (see step 4 below).

Thread the needle again as before, and take it around the head of the tassel, pass it through the loop, pull it up tightly and secure it by pushing the needle up through the head and out at the top of the tassel (see step 5 below).

Do not cut off these threads as they can be used to sew the tassel in place (see step 6 below). For a thicker tassel, use more threads.

Tassels made of yarn matching that used in a design will enhance the end product.

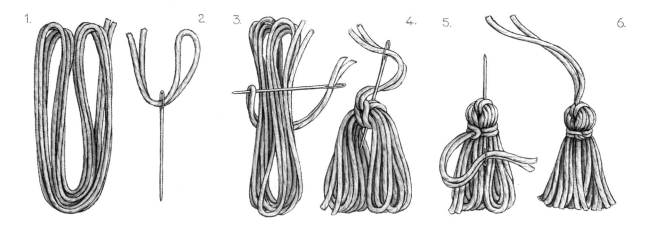

making your own gift or greetings card

Divide the piece of cardboard into three equal sections. The middle section will have the window cut from it.

Cut a piece of thin white or coloured cardboard 15 × 33cm (6 × 13½in).

Lightly score the card to divide it into three sections (see right), each 11cm (4½in) wide. Then fold along the scored lines.

The lefthand section becomes the back of the card, the middle section is the front of the card and the righthand section folds over the back of the card front to neaten it.

Carefully mark and then cut out your chosen 'window' shape, using a sharp craft knife. Make sure the hole you cut is centrally positioned.

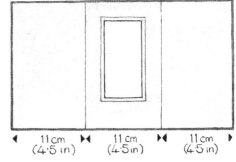

If using a circular shape, you may wish to place it nearer the top of the card than the bottom to give a more pleasing effect.

covering a curtain ring

A small crochet hook can be used to cover a curtain ring with thread.
1. Make a slip loop and pass the hook into it. Hold the curtain ring between your left thumb and forefinger.

2. Pass the hook through the ring, picking up the yarn and drawing it back through the ring. Then pass the hook over the ring, pick up the yarn and draw it back through the two loops.

Use a crochet hook and yarn to cover a curtain ring.

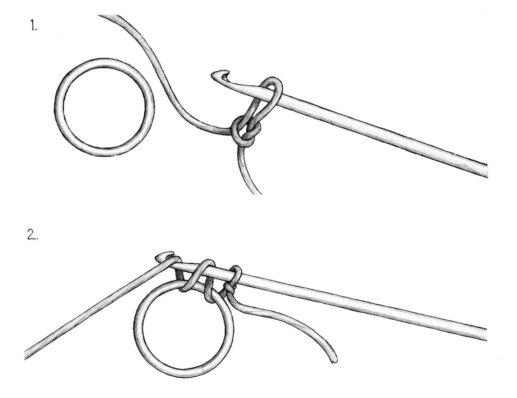

1.

2.

3.

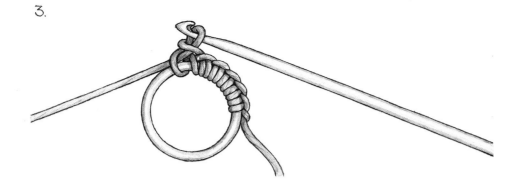

3.   Repeat this until the ring is well covered. Cut the yarn, leaving a tail which can be used to sew the ring in position.

finishing tips

All the projects in the book include instructions for finishing your embroidery. Generally, you should always remember to handle your stitchery with care, so that the fabric looks fresh and requires the minimum of pressing (if any).

If you do have to press your embroidery, *never* do so on the right side, as it will flatten and spoil the texture and finish of your stitchery. Always press on the wrong side, preferably with a steam iron.

Light use of spray starch can be effective.

If you need to lace your embroidery over a board to make a picture, remember to allow plenty of fabric around each edge of the design area for it to be folded over to the wrong side. Use cardboard that will not bend easily and strong button thread that will not break when pulled tightly.

damp-stretching

All of the projects given are worked with the use of a frame or hoop, so the need to damp-stretch finished work should not arise. However, occasionally you will find that fabric or canvas may become distorted during embroidery, and damp-stretching will be necessary to get it back into shape.

Everything must be colourfast and shrink-resistant and you should only use the minimum of water.

Place several layers of white blotting paper on an old board and dampen them. Then place the embroidery (right side upwards) on top. The moisture from the paper dampens the fabric, making it supple and thus allowing you to stretch it more easily. Use rust-free drawing pins (thumb tacks) to hold the embroidery in position. Gently pull and stretch the fabric back into its correct shape, working with opposite sides from the centres to the corners. You may find that you have to adjust the pins in order to achieve the correct shape.

Leave the stretched fabric on the board to dry in a warm atmosphere. Then release the fabric and you will see that the distorted shape has been rectified.

Remember that you must have plenty of excess fabric around the embroidered area into which the drawing pins (tacks) are placed, as they will probably leave small holes which can spoil the fabric.

care of embroidery

If you have used good quality fabric and threads, your embroidery will last for years and years.

However, there are certain ways of prolonging the life of stitchery. Never place any embroidery in direct sunlight or near strong artificial lights, as both heat and light cause colours to fade and the fibres of fabrics and threads to weaken. Similarly, do not place embroidery near a heat source, as this will also make the stitchery very brittle. Remember, too, that a damp atmosphere can be equally damaging.

Frequent laundering should be avoided if at all possible and always use a mild cleaning agent. Gently reshape the article while damp and do not allow it to dry out completely before pressing it on the wrong side with a steam iron.

If you need to clean a cushion or some other article that may not be totally colourfast, then dry cleaning is essential. You will find that if you treat your embroidered articles with loving care and respect, they will require little more than a gentle brush and shake, or the use of the curtain attachment of the vacuum cleaner carefully held over them, to remove dust.

Care for your embroidery as though it is an heirloom in the making. Enjoy it, respect it, but equally do not hide it away. Folding it and sealing it in a plastic bag will cause permanent creases which will in time weaken and break. Also, the lack of air will prevent the fibres from breathing. If you must store your work for a long period of time, it is better if it can be stored flat or rolled smoothly (right side out), in layers of protective, acid-free tissue paper. Then it should be placed in a clean fabric cover such as a pillowcase, and finally placed somewhere dark, dry and, of course, moth-free.

stockists and suppliers

Binney and Smith (Europe) Ltd
Ampthill Road
Bedford MK42 9RS
(Crayola fabric transfer crayons)

Coats Domestic Marketing Division
39 Durham Street
Glasgow G41 1BS
(full range of Anchor embroidery threads, information and lists of stockists)

Dunlicraft Ltd
Pullman Road
Wigston
Leicester LE8 2DY
(DMC threads, information and lists of stockists)

John Lewis
Oxford Street
London W1A 1EX
(cotton fabrics, towelling, bed linen)

Liberty
210–220 Regent Street
London W1R 6AH
(plain and patterned cotton fabrics)

M.P. Stonehouse Ltd
NeedleArt House
P.O. Box 13
Albion Mills
Wakefield
West Yorkshire WF2 9SG
(Paterna Persian wools)

C. M. Offray and Son Ltd
Fir Tree Place
Church Road
Ashford
Middlesex TW15 2PH
(ribbons)

H. W. Peel and Co. Ltd
Norwester House
Fairway Drive
Greenford
Middlesex UB6 8PW
(Chartwell metric pattern guide paper
– squared and graph)

The following addresses may be of use
to American readers.

Susan Bates
212 Middlesex Avenue
Chester, Connecticut 06412
(distributor for Anchor embroidery
threads)

Binney and Smith Inc.
Consumer Affairs Department
P.O. Box 431
Easton, Pennsylvania 18044
(Crayola fabric transfer crayons)

DMC Corporation
107 Trumbull Street
Elizabeth, New Jersey 07206
(DMC threads, information and lists
of stockists)

Johnson Creative Arts
445 Main Street
West Townend
Massachussetts 01474
(distributor for Paterna Persian
wools)

acknowledgements

Acknowledgements are due to so many people who have helped and encouraged me during the creation of *The Needlework Garden* that it is impossible to mention everyone by name.

Thanks to all the friends of Jackie Boase, who so enthusiastically let us invade their beautiful homes and gardens in Suffolk to photograph each piece of embroidery in a sympathetic setting. In particular Julie Coley, Sue Day, Jane Sheppard, Carmel Sturridge, Mary Taylor and Sue Warner. Also thanks to Jackie Boase for the care and attention with which she styled each setting so that every piece of embroidery was quietly complemented; and for welcoming the 'team' into her home during the photographic sessions. To Julie Fisher and her tireless assistants, for the stunning photography. To Cherriwyn Magill, for her attention to detail and precision in designing the book. To Sally Holmes, for the beautiful artwork, of which every single drawing is exquisitely and painstakingly carried out. I would also like to thank Mike Hutton, Cara Whigham and Elsie Shevas of Dunlicraft Limited, who are always so helpful whenever a request for fabrics and threads is made by me. Thanks to Jane Judd, my agent, who helped me develop the initial idea. A special thanks to Sarah Wallace for her enthusiastic belief in *The Needlework Garden* and also to Valerie Buckingham for all her encouragement. Finally, to Dan, thank you for all your patience and support.

The author and the publishers are grateful to the following companies which supplied materials for the projects in the book: Dunlicraft Limited for DMC stranded embroidery thread, coton perlé, tapisserie wool and soft embroidery cotton; also for Zweigart fabrics and canvas. J & P Coats (UK) Limited for stranded embroidery thread, coton perlé and tapisserie wool; NeedleArt House for Paterna Persian wools; C. M. Offray & Son Limited for ribbons.

index

DATE DUE